You CAN Eat That!

Awesome Food for Kids with Diabetes

Robyn Webb, M.S.

You **CAN** Eat That! Awesome Food for Kids with Diabetes

Cleveland Clinic Press

Contact:

Cleveland Clinic Press

9500 Euclid Avenue NA 32, Cleveland, Ohio 44195

216-445-5547

delongk@ccf.org

www.clevelandclinicpress.org

This book is not intended to replace personal medical care and supervision. There is no substitute for the experience and information that a child's doctor can provide. Rather, it is our hope that this book will offer additional resources to parents seeking information on nutrition for children with diabetes.

Proper medical care should be tailored to the individual patient. If you read something in this book that seems to conflict with instructions given by your child's doctor, contact the doctor. Since each case is different, there may be good reasons for individual treatment to differ from the information presented in this book.

If you have questions about any treatment or practice mentioned in this book, consult your doctor.

Library of Congress Cataloging-in-Publication Data

Webb, Robyn.

You CAN Eat That! Awesome Food for Kids with Diabetes / by Robyn Webb.

p. cm.

Includes bibliographical references and index.

ISBN 978-1-59624-029-2 (alk. paper)

1. Diabetes in children--Diet therapy--Recipes. I. Title.

RJ420.D5W43 2007   641.5'6314083--dc22

2007023045

Cover concept by Tanner Johnson • Book design by Whitney Campbell

Photography by Steve Travarca, Cleveland Clinic Center for Medical Art and Photography

Dedication

To all children with diabetes –
I applaud your courage and strength.
You are all awesome.

Contents

Acknowledgments

No book is ever created by just one person, and many people were instrumental in the creation of this work. Thanks are due especially to the following:

Kids first! From small to tall, each of these children served as a great taste-tester – there's nothing like the honesty that comes from children. To sisters Rachel and Rebecca Volentine and the French/Obenauer children, Erin, Brianna, Ian, Zoe, Brittany, and Alexander: Thank you! I know you had lots of fun trying all the foods!

To my chief testers, Bobbie McConnell (mother of Rachel and Rebecca), Barbara and Dirk French (parents of the French/Obenauer children), and Liz Porter (Barbara and Dirk's neighbor), thank you.

To the Jones family of the Chef's Garden and Culinary Vegetable Institute in Huron, Ohio, goes my great appreciation for the opportunity to shoot our photos at their marvelous facility. Equal gratitude is due Chef Greg Klaus, whose beautifully prepared and styled dishes appear throughout the pages of this book.

To my publicist and agent, Beth Shepard, for your undying commitment to me and my work. Your support over the many years has never gone unrecognized. Thanks for believing in me.

To Cleveland Clinic Press go thanks for the vision to establish a publishing group at one of the finest medical centers in our country. I was deeply flattered when I was chosen to create this much-needed book for kids with diabetes. To recognize that we must teach our children well from an early age shows great insight.

Preface

Your child has been diagnosed with diabetes and you feel as if your world has been turned upside down. Parents commonly feel some responsibility and guilt over their children's development of diabetes. Parents naturally and instinctively want to protect their children from harm, so when a child develops a chronic illness that has no cure, it's common to wonder what could have been done to avoid it.

The first thing you need to know is that there was nothing you could have done to prevent the onset of your child's type 1 diabetes. The good news is that you and your child can successfully adjust to life with this disease. With knowledge, determination, and diligent medical care, a child with diabetes should be able to lead a healthy, active, and happy life.

Insulin injections, blood tests, and medical exams can be extremely hard on a child as well as on the parents. But I believe that besides the medical issues, one of the most difficult things for families to deal with is also one of the most common daily experiences: eating. It's difficult enough to prepare meals for picky eaters. When you throw diabetes into the mix, the picture becomes much more complicated.

Parents may not realize that there are many ways to retain the joy of eating and preparing great meals. If you feel limited by your choices, you simply may need a little fresh inspiration and some new ideas about how to cope with your child's diabetes. This book is aimed at giving you fantastic ideas and recipes so that your child can still be "part of the gang." You'll learn how to balance diabetes control with nutritious food that tastes great and actually appeals to children.

Food should be creative and fun for kids, too. If children learn early on that food is something to be enjoyed, mealtimes will be much more pleasant for the entire family. Having diabetes does not mean that your child should settle for bland, boring food. The recipes offered here are easy to prepare from common ingredients. Most important, they're all "kid-tested" and geared particularly to kids' tastes. Now there will be no need for you to prepare separate meals. All these recipes were tested among children with diabetes – as well as children without – and it was unanimous: The food was tasty for everyone!

One of my goals when planning this book was to expand the use of vegetables and fruits used in a food plan in a "kid-friendly" way. In speaking with numerous parents, I learned that getting children to eat their greens could be quite a challenge. In fact, of the children who sampled these recipes, several said they really disliked many fruits and vegetables. Others thought fruit and veggies were "blah." After all, unlike the many alluring products kids see on television, a piece of fruit doesn't come in a colorful box or with a toy. With the recipes provided here, these children not only ate their portions but really liked the flavors of the fruits and vegetables used. When I asked them why, the consensus was that all the ingredients were "just combined right." Merely placing a side of boiled carrots on your child's plate doesn't work. So fruits and vegetables are used creatively in each chapter to encourage your child to want to eat these foods.

Another one of my goals was to keep the food low in fat. We know that the incidence of childhood obesity is rising rapidly. We also know that for children with diabetes who are overweight, losing weight becomes even more critical in the fight to keep diabetes under control. I used low-fat food products in recipes, but I never compromised on the taste. Believe me, the children were quite vocal about that! And if a recipe tasted "too fake," as one child succinctly put it, the recipe was reworked until both nutrition and flavor got a green light.

Children today are subjected to far too much saturated fat, which can complicate their diabetes care. But you'll notice that not every smidgen of fat is removed from the recipes. Your child still needs some fats – the good, monounsaturated kind, like olive oil.

Then there's the issue of sugar. The taste of sweets naturally appeals to children (and to most people, I might add), so I did include recipes using sweeteners. For the best results, the no-calorie sweetener Splenda® was used because it measures and sweetens in the same way that sugar does. But wherever possible, I tried to rely on the natural sweetness of fruit or spices like cinnamon. The earlier children's palates can be trained to enjoy naturally sweet flavors, the easier time parents have keeping them off large amounts of sweets. But whether the subject is sugar or fat, the one word I can't stress enough is "moderation."

So the next time you plan a consultation with a registered dietitian, bring this recipe book to your appointment. A registered dietitian will know how to incorporate these recipes into the plan designed for your child. There is no doubt that planning meals and finding the right foods to manage your child's diabetes can be overwhelming. It is my hope that when you incorporate some of these recipes into your daily routine, your child will not only feel like everyone else in the family but may even be inspired to become the family cook!

Introduction

Basic understanding of diabetes management for kids

Imagine this scenario: Your child has just been diagnosed with diabetes and you're meeting with a health-care professional. When the discussion turns to food, you're prepared for the worst. Among the misconceptions you may have is that your child can never have sweets again, your child will have to eat chicken and steamed vegetables forever, and you might as well forget about eating out at restaurants ever again. You clench your teeth, squeeze your eyes shut, and brace yourself. But suddenly you relax when you're told that sweets in moderation can be okay, that your child can eat favorite foods, and that you can go ahead and make that dinner reservation.

Just as recently as the past five to seven years, the food choices for adults and children with diabetes have expanded greatly, allowing for a more realistic (and flavorful) way to manage the disease. While some choices are clearly better than others, the emphasis is on the word "choice." The restricted world of bland, boring food no longer composes the entire menu for people with diabetes.

In general, the major key to managing childhood diabetes is learning how to control blood sugar. There are three basic rules to achieve this. They are:

- Give your child's body the chemical it needs (insulin) to better process the sugars that are naturally there.
- Develop lifestyle habits for your child that include sufficient exercise, relaxation, sleep, and vitamin supplements, all of which make our bodies far less susceptible or sensitive to blood-sugar swings.
- Adjust your child's diet to make sure that the right nutrients are included in a way that won't cause big surges in blood sugar.

That last point is what this cookbook is all about – learning how to prepare and serve healthful, delicious, well-balanced foods that act as a defense against blood-sugar surges in our children. The big bonus is that with an improved diet, many children will lose excess weight, which is also a key to good blood-sugar management.

Not long ago, the recommended diabetic diet forbade sugar and severely restricted carbohydrates and fats. Today we know that people with diabetes can eat a wide variety of foods if they're put together in a plan that, consistently practiced, can give your child better control over the disease.

Once you've met with a dietitian to discuss your child's blood-sugar goals, it will be up to you and your child to keep the daily blood-sugar readings as even as possible. Some children will manage their diabetes simply by eating healthful foods and cutting down on empty calories, while others need a more detailed program. Whatever regimen you need to follow, the goal is the same: keeping the blood-sugar level from going out of control.

How a registered dietitian can help

Your child with diabetes will spend countless hours consulting with health-care professionals, and with good reason. Although the ultimate responsibility for managing your child's diabetes lies with your child and the immediate family, a good health-care team, which includes a trained dietitian, is invaluable. With information about diabetes care continually changing, the challenge for you and your child to keep up with all of it is overwhelming. That's where a registered dietitian can help. An authority on the role of food in health, the RD plays a vital role on the health-care team by providing specific expertise about food and nutrition.

To become a registered dietitian, an individual must complete at least four years of education in nutrition or a related field at an accredited college or university. Completion of a supervised internship also may be required. A potential candidate must then pass an extensive examination given by the Commission on Dietetic Registration, the credentialing agency of the American Dietetic Association. Afterward, the RD must maintain status by completing seventy-five hours of continuing education every five years.

The dietitian will help you and your child with meal planning and will develop a plan based on your child's food preferences. An RD can also help teach you and your child how to handle parties, holidays, after-school activities, and travel. It's likely that you'll be asked to keep records that note everything your child drinks and eats. This will help you establish your child's correct insulin program and will enable you to discover eating patterns that need adjusting. Use the RD effectively by asking questions about terminology that may not seem clear to you or your child.

If your child is also overweight, a dietitian can design an appropriate weight-loss program. Be prepared to share your child's eating habits, adverse reactions to food, weight history, general medical history, and any previous nutrition counseling you may have received. The more information you can provide about your child's dietary status, the better prepared the RD will be to assist you. There are many issues involved in the care of your child's diabetes, but with the support of a professionally trained RD, you'll be able to successfully see your child through the difficult times as well as the good ones.

Carbohydrates: Friends or foes?

Carbohydrates come in many forms and in many foods. Carbohydrates have the greatest impact on blood-sugar levels. Refined or simple carbohydrates are so easy to digest that they flood the body with blood sugar. If that's the case, the question is: Is it advisable to cut back on carbohydrates?

At first glance, it would seem to make sense. In fact, even the American Diabetes Association says that there are some people who do need to lower their carbohydrate intake in order to better manage their diabetes. At the same time, however, it's widely recognized by most of the medical community that following a strict low-carbohydrate food program may do more harm than good. And for children to follow a restrictive program usually spells disaster. Children need carbohydrates for the energy they burn.

So what role do carbohydrates play, and why are they important in controlling blood sugar? We can't expect children to feel energetic and full of pep if they don't consume carbohydrates. And since carbohydrates make up about half the calories of fat per gram, a food program that includes carbohydrates also gives your child wider food choices. These alone are two very good reasons that carbohydrates shouldn't be looked upon as the "bad guys."

Many of the popular low-carb diets don't differentiate adequately between types of carbs: Are they the bagel-type carbs or the broccoli-type? There's a big difference, yet many of those plans limit all carbohydrates, regardless of the source. Even in the case of children with diabetes, for whom blood-sugar management is essential, there's nothing really wrong with sugar except that for the most part sweets are accompanied by fat and lack many vitamins or minerals. Sweets certainly can be eaten, but they need to be eaten in smaller quantities.

Then there are the starches, better known as complex carbohydrates. These are full of fiber. Most Americans, whether or not they have diabetes, don't consume the recommended daily amount of fiber. Yet fiber is exactly what will help control blood-sugar levels. So fill your child's plate with vegetables, whole grains, and beans.

Fiber takes up space in the stomach and small intestine, where it absorbs water and slows down digestion enough to prolong feelings of satiation. It's extremely important to the maintenance of proper blood-sugar levels. Since fluctuating blood-sugar levels influence feelings of hunger and irritability as well as energy levels, high-fiber foods such as vegetables, whole grains, and beans also help to keep your child on a more even keel.

Consequently, there's no need to follow a faddish low-carbohydrate plan to control your child's diabetes. Foods high in complex carbohydrates help control one of the most important factors in diabetes management – the ability to manage blood sugar while maintaining high energy levels and reaping the benefits of the many vitamins and minerals they provide.

Fond of fat?

Happily, not all fat is bad, and there is solid evidence that eating some fat is beneficial for a child with diabetes. Fat slows the digestion, causing sugar to enter the bloodstream gradually – a goal of blood-sugar control. And there is evidence that monounsaturated fat raises the HDL cholesterol (the good one). This is important for people with diabetes because they run an increased risk of heart disease. Even when very young, children can have high levels of cholesterol, and the sooner high cholesterol is managed, the better it will be for your child's diabetes.

Also, monounsaturated fat has been shown in some research to reduce insulin resistance, allowing for better blood-sugar control. While fat isn't evil, it's not perfect either. You'll still need to watch out for how much and what kind of fat your child eats. For the best sources of monounsaturated fat, try to stick with small amounts of olive oil, canola oil, avocados, and certain nuts, such as almonds.

How much protein is enough?

Protein also plays a role in blood-sugar control, but it's digested more slowly than carbohydrates and it causes a more gradual rise in blood-sugar levels. Loading your child's plate with steak and hamburger, however, isn't the answer.

Fortunately, a true protein deficiency doesn't really exist among the people of developed countries. We get plenty of protein. It's in many foods, even in vegetables and grains, which are really carbohydrates first. Your child can meet all necessary protein needs through animal and non-animal sources – everything from meat, poultry, and fish to beans, nuts, and soy products. Another reason not to go overboard with protein is that you can significantly cut down the amount of saturated fat you consume when you say goodbye to higher-fat cuts of meat, chicken skin, excess butter, and high-fat dairy products.

Planning meals

Once you understand your child's needs, you'll find it best to plan meals around meeting those needs. Why plan? Many of us think about dinner on the way home from work or minutes before we walk through the door. But your child's needs make that impractical. Planning will help you manage your child's diabetes by keeping your diet organized and consistent.

Even so, planning ahead doesn't need to be too restrictive or stressful. In fact, the opposite is true; planning takes the angst out of having to make last-minute suggestions that can throw you off your child's health goals. It's when you're too tired or the pantry is empty that you put your child's diabetes in jeopardy. Through simple planning, you can be in control.

There are many ways to plan meals. Gone are the days of a set of preprinted menus. By using the exchange system, carbohydrate-counting, or calorie-counting, you have many options for including a wide variety of foods in your diet each day. With any one of these systems in place, your child has the freedom to eat out, have a slice of cake or a scoop of ice cream, or choose never to eat lima beans again.

Your child's written plan becomes like a food diary. It will help you to see the interaction of food, exercise, and medication as well as the effect they have on blood-sugar levels. Through planning, you'll come to know whether your child needs a snack at 4 p.m. or whether one at 10 a.m. would be better. Planning will help you determine how much insulin to use and whether your child should eat sooner or later. What your child eats raises blood sugar, and by tracking you can adjust exercise and medications, which lower it. Keeping track of what your child eats is definitely worth the time it takes.

A good way to begin to plan is to meet with a registered dietitian to discuss your child's food likes and dislikes. The RD can help you determine the types of foods your child can eat and help you make a schedule of what your child should eat and when.

Each child's situation is unique. By using a meal-planning system, you can deal with such considerations as after-school sports or family trips and successfully meet the food needs of everyone in the family while taking into account their food allergies and your food budget.

Perhaps you'll want to use your computer to help you plan. Whatever method you choose, it's a much more organized approach to write down your child's plan, rather than keep it in your head. You'll meet your child's diabetes-management goals much better if you have a written plan to which you can refer. And it will serve as a log if you need to reformulate your plan.

Promoting healthy eating

It's very important for kids of all ages to be part of a group and accepted by their peers. This is especially so when your child has a busy social calendar, because eating with peers can be difficult. Even though your child's meal plan can be flexible enough to include a dessert or other favorite food, there are times you'll want your child to refrain from eating certain foods in order to maintain better glucose control.

The best approach to healthful eating is to figure out a way for your child to have a desired food item while keeping blood sugar under control. If your child feels deprived or different from everyone else, it can cause long-term resentment and resistance to diabetes management.

When you're planning meals and making decisions about what to serve, try to include your child in the selection process. As your child grows older and learns more about diabetes, understanding the food groups and the effect of different foods on blood glucose will be important. Teaching and reinforcing this will take some time and patience, but eventually your child will be able to decide between a cookie and a pretzel, and know how to adjust medications, activity levels, and meal times accordingly.

When other children are present, strive to make your child's food as similar as possible. Substitute a broiled hamburger (where much of the fat has drained away) and pretzels for a fried hamburger and potato chips. At home, it's helpful if everyone eats the same meal. It's neither recommended nor necessary to serve a separate meal to a child with diabetes.

You may want to enlist "helper" adults who can support your child in making healthful food choices away from home. At school, talk to your child's teacher or other staff members who may be familiar with diabetes and who can assist your child in making the right food choices.

And keep communication flowing. Ask your child to let you know when a desire for sweets becomes irresistible. That way you can adjust insulin intake.

Work with a dietitian to develop a flexible program that will include foods your child truly loves. This may prevent your child from binge-eating or sneaking food. Don't make it seem forced or artificial, but always offer your child positive reinforcement for successfully following the meal plan.

Preventing low blood sugar

One of the most common problems for children with diabetes is hypoglycemia, or low blood sugar. Hypoglycemia usually can be easily treated with a small amount of sweets. However, when the balance of insulin, food, and exercise is disrupted by schedule conflicts, illness, and so on, blood-glucose levels can drop too low. This can be dangerous for anyone with diabetes, and it's especially scary for children.

Make sure your child eats on time and follows a regular schedule of insulin injections. A snack before exercise also can help prevent lows. Sometimes it's difficult to recognize the symptoms of low blood sugar. In fact, they may be different each time. Symptoms can range from misbehavior and crankiness to sleepiness and unresponsiveness. In severe cases, seizures and unconsciousness can occur.

It's important to teach your child to communicate with you whenever strange or uncomfortable feelings occur. It's equally important to ensure that teachers and any other adults who may have contact with your child can recognize the symptoms of hypoglycemia.

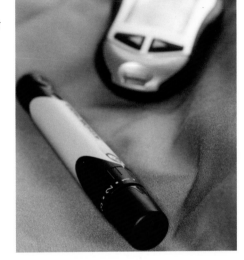

The best way to know whether the blood sugar is indeed low is to monitor it with a glucometer. If a meter is not available and your child is alert and able to swallow, administer food or drink. Have your child get into the habit of carrying around one or two glucose tablets, a few Lifesavers, and a few small gumdrops. (You can carry them if you're with your child for much of the day.) At home keep orange or apple juice (½ cup) or honey (one or two tablespoons) on hand. Any of these should bring the blood sugar up, after which you can follow the first treatment with a few crackers topped with about one tablespoon of peanut butter or one ounce of hard cheese. The important thing to remember is not to overtreat. It doesn't take a lot of pure sugar to bring the blood-sugar level back to normal.

Avoiding diabetes burnout

Although this is essentially a cookbook, I'd like to note the important role that emotions play when you're dealing with diabetes. You've worked so hard to care for your child's diabetes – you've carefully shopped for food, made sure your child is getting insulin on time, talked to all the other adults affected by your child's diabetes – and now all you want is to take a good long nap. Diabetes burnout happens to the most diligent and caring of parents. Without some plan for staying sane while you're working to keep your child healthy, diabetes burnout is sure to find you eventually.

Don't allow the weight of the world to settle on your shoulders alone. Diabetes care is a partnership. Everyone needs to be involved in it: the child, you, your spouse or significant other, and the other kids in the household. Break up routine care into individual tasks that can be divided among family members. Also, be sure to have your child tell you what help other family members can provide.

Cut yourself some slack when it comes to striving for perfect health goals. Your child's blood-sugar levels don't have to be exactly on target at every single reading. This is particularly so when your child becomes a teen and experiences hormonal and emotional changes that affect the blood-sugar levels. Agree on goals that are "good enough": goals that keep your child well and healthy, and you sane.

Let it all hang out! Feelings, that is. Diabetes can produce anger, resentment, frustration, and lots of stress. Children should have the room to acknowledge their feelings about having diabetes. We don't want to discount those feelings by telling them that diabetes really isn't so bad. To them it *is* bad! Children know how they feel. Feeling bad about diabetes is natural and normal. As much as you want to protect your child from all things, feelings need to be expressed, accepted, and dealt with. Just listen with lots of love.

Don't forget that you have feelings, too. Children can have a tough time adhering to their food plans. They may insist on eating foods that really send their blood sugar into a tailspin. Instead of blaming your child for self-destructive behavior, make sure you communicate how you feel. Don't be afraid to let your child know that this kind of behavior makes you feel scared or frustrated.

Depending on the age of your child, expressing your own feelings will have varying degrees of success. Even though you may not immediately succeed in getting your child to go back to eating properly, at least you won't drive the child away. And everything will be out in the open. Your honesty can serve as a model for your child, who also needs to learn how to deal with feelings of anger and frustration effectively.

Also make sure that you're receiving proper support from your child's diabetes health-care team and that they always check weight, height, and blood pressure. An A1C test, which determines average blood sugar over a period of eight to twelve weeks, should be performed about every three months. For people with diabetes it's best if that value falls below 7.0. Numbers higher than 7.0 may indicate that blood-sugar control needs better management.

Blood lipids, kidney function, and eyes also need to be checked regularly. These tests allow you to get a long-term sense of how well the blood sugar is being controlled and enable you to monitor for potential problems. Use your health-care team as much as makes you feel comfortable. Be sure your team includes not only a physician but also a registered dietitian who knows kids and understands children's needs.

If you're not getting what you think you need, speak up. Make sure you have a team whose members listen to your questions and are willing to research questions they can't answer. The right health-care team is an invaluable tool for managing your child's diabetes.

Helping your child live with diabetes

There will come a time when your child grows up and assumes sole responsibility for managing the diabetes. Although a diabetes health-care team is very important, diabetes is managed in the real world: at home, on the soccer field, or at a party. Before your child reaches adulthood, small steps and then gradually larger ones should be taken to turn your child into an independent adult capable of dealing with matters related to health.

Keep in mind that your job is to help your child learn to control blood-sugar levels; you can't control them yourself. Your child will want to be as unencumbered by diabetes as possible. Your job is to support, not to push. You need to sympathize, help solve problems, and keep from being too critical. Children should not necessarily make diabetes-management decisions all on their own, but parents must help them take the lead in making those decisions.

A useful technique for problem-solving is to ask your child questions such as "What are you having the most difficult time with now in managing your diabetes?" or "What specifically can I do to help?" Ask real questions, be sympathetic, and show genuine concern. Ask questions designed to foster communication between you and your child. And learn from success. Ask your child why something worked so well. By understanding what went right in a situation that usually goes wrong, the two of you can uncover important information about long-term diabetes control.

Keep in mind that any issue is easier when you break it down into steps. Think of a situation you want to work on with your child. Perhaps it's getting your child to self-administer the shots. Think of all the steps involved in the process. A way to begin to help your child to become more independent is to delegate one or two steps in the process. Perhaps your child can get out the insulin and then put everything away after the shot is taken.

Passing on the responsibility to the child for taking care of the diabetes builds confidence, ensures that the diabetes care is being managed successfully, and strengthens the parent-child relationship. Stay involved with your child and check regularly to see how things are going.

A child who has diabetes has to do many things that other children don't have to do and has to make many decisions that other children don't have to make. Children with diabetes learn the importance of being disciplined and taking responsibility for themselves. While no one would choose to have diabetes in order to learn these things, learning to live successfully with diabetes can be an experience that ultimately enriches your child's life.

Awesome Recipes

SUPER SOUPS

Soup is a wonderful way of adding nutrition to your child's diet. Unfortunately, in addition to being high in sodium and fat, canned soups lose many of their vitamins in the canning process. So in terms of nutrition it pays to make your soups from scratch with vitamin- and fiber-rich vegetables. Although most of the recipes make four to six servings, the nice thing about soup is that you can easily double or triple the recipes and freeze portions for later use. If you make different soups and freeze them, you'll always have a handy choice when time is tight. You'll discover that the extra effort is worth it.

Accompanied by a salad and whole-grain bread, the soups in this chapter can be the main meal, or they can be served as a light snack or appetizer. You'll see how easy it is to add flavor by using herbs and spices and other ingredients that are devoid of excess fat, sugar, or sodium. And the addition of beans and plenty of vegetables keeps the fiber content high.

"Eye appeal" is also important. Think of those food packages with photos of "serving suggestions," and then look at your own dishes. You can do that, too. To make a soup even more attractive for your child, why not gussy it up a bit with a great garnish? Reduced-fat shredded cheese for bean or vegetable soups makes a nourishing topping. A dollop of nonfat sour cream adds contrast in texture and temperature to many soups. Even tossing in a spoonful of popped corn makes a fun way to get your child to eat soup. You can also get children involved by asking them to provide their own creative finishing touches.

Most of the soups in this chapter can be covered and refrigerated for three or four days. Many of the soups also can be frozen. To freeze soup, first let it come to room temperature and then refrigerate it for a few hours. At that point, transfer the soup to a large freezer bag or container, leaving half an inch of headspace for expansion. Frozen soup will keep for about three months. Ideally, you'll let the frozen soup thaw overnight in the refrigerator and then reheat it gently. If necessary, add a little water or broth to thin.

Soup should be brimming with good nutrition as well as flavor. And with these great soup recipes, you'll have all that goodness in one little bowl. Use these recipes as a springboard and you, too, can become a "souper" star with your family.

AMAZING ALPHABET SOUP

Serves: 6
Serving size: 1 cup
Preparation time: 20 minutes
Cooking time: 30 minutes

Ingredients

2 teaspoons olive oil

½ medium-size red onion, peeled and finely diced

2 garlic cloves, peeled and minced

1 boneless, skinless chicken breast, cut into small pieces

2 cans (14 oz.) diced tomatoes, drained

6 cups low-fat, reduced-sodium chicken broth

½ cup dry alphabet pasta, or other pasta, such as rotelle (wagon wheels)

Salt and pepper to taste

ABCs are easy to love in this hearty pasta soup. But ABC can become ASAP any time of year by substituting any fun-shaped pasta offered seasonally at most local grocers.

1 Heat the oil in a large saucepan over medium-high heat. Add the red onion, garlic, and chicken and cook about 5 minutes, stirring occasionally, until the chicken is cooked through.

2 Add the remaining ingredients and bring to a boil. Reduce the heat to medium-low and cook at a low boil for 7 to 9 minutes, stirring occasionally, until the pasta is tender. Season to taste with salt and pepper before serving.

NUTRITION PER SERVING

Calories 191
Calories from fat 34
Total fat 4g
    Saturated fat 1g
Cholesterol 47mg
Sodium 233mg
Carbohydrate 22g
    Dietary fiber 3g
    Sugars 5g
Protein 17.5g

CHUNKY, CHUNKY (DID WE SAY CHUNKY?) BEEF SOUP

Your family may rave over your roasts, but leftovers often raise an eyebrow. Don't despair. Take that beef, mix in some veggies and orzo, and you have the perfect chunky soup for a cold winter night. It's comfort food at its chunky best.

Serves: 4

Serving size: 1 cup

Preparation time: 20 minutes

Cooking time: 40 minutes

Ingredients

2   teaspoons olive oil

2   medium-size carrots, peeled and diced

1   large celery stalk, trimmed and diced

1   small onion, peeled and diced

1   small zucchini, trimmed and diced

4   cups low-fat, reduced-sodium beef broth

1   can (14 oz.) diced tomatoes, drained

⅓ cup dry orzo

1   cup cooked beef (left over from a steak or roast), cut into bite-size pieces

Salt and pepper to taste

1 Heat the oil in a large, heavy saucepan over medium–high heat. Add the carrots, celery, onion, and zucchini and cook about 6 minutes until softened, stirring occasionally. Stir in the broth and tomatoes and bring to a boil. Reduce the heat to low and simmer for 10 minutes.

2 Stir in the orzo and cook 6 to 8 minutes at a low simmer until tender. Add the beef, season with salt and pepper, and continue to cook on low for about 5 minutes until the beef is heated through. Serve immediately.

NUTRITION PER SERVING

Calories 190
Calories from fat 56
Total fat 6g
    Saturated fat 2g
Cholesterol 19mg
Sodium 219mg
Carbohydrate 17g
    Dietary fiber 2g
    Sugars 5g
Protein 16g

SHE SERVES SASSY-SAUCY SAUSAGE SOUP

Easier to make than it is to say, this saucy sausage soup can be ready in practically no time at all. Serve it with crunchy Crispy Cheese Crackers (page 140) for a tongue-twistingly complete dinner.

Serves: 4

Serving size: 1 cup

Preparation time: 30 minutes

Cooking time: 15 minutes

Ingredients

4 oz. mild or spicy lean bulk Italian turkey sausage

1 small red bell pepper, cored, seeded, and sliced

1 medium-size onion, peeled and diced

2 garlic cloves, peeled and minced

3 cups low-fat, reduced-sodium chicken broth

1 can (14 oz.) chopped tomatoes

2 medium-size red potatoes, peeled and cut into 1-inch cubes

1 teaspoon dried basil

Salt and pepper to taste

1 In a large, heavy saucepan over medium heat, fry the sausage, stirring and crumbling it as you go, for 2 minutes. Add the red pepper, onion, and garlic and cook about 4 minutes, stirring occasionally, until the peppers and onion are tender.

2 Add the broth, tomatoes, and potatoes, and bring to a boil. Reduce the heat to medium-low, cover, and simmer for 10 minutes until the potatoes are tender. Stir in the basil, salt, and pepper, and cook for 2 minutes more before serving.

NUTRITION
PER SERVING

Calories 130
Calories from fat 34
Total fat 4g
 Saturated fat 1.5g
Cholesterol 34mg
Sodium 440mg
Carbohydrate 15g
 Dietary fiber 3g
 Sugars 6g
Protein 10g

COSMIC CHILI

Get a blast out of this protein-packed chili. It's lower in fat than traditional chili and it still explodes with flavor. You can fire it up even more, if you like, by adding more chili powder.

Serves: 6

Serving size: 1 cup

Preparation time: 30 minutes

Cooking time: 30 minutes

Ingredients

1 tablespoon olive oil

1 pound lean ground turkey

1 medium-size onion, peeled and diced

1 medium-size green bell pepper, cored, seeded, and diced

2 garlic cloves, peeled and minced

1 tablespoon chili powder (or more to taste)

1 teaspoon ground cumin

1 can (28 oz.) can crushed tomatoes

1 can (14 oz.) kidney beans, drained and rinsed

Salt and pepper to taste

½ cup reduced-fat shredded cheddar cheese

1 Heat the oil in a large, heavy saucepan over medium-high heat. Add the turkey and cook about 5 minutes until browned, stirring to break up any lumps. Drain off all but 1 teaspoon of the oil.

2 Add the onion, green pepper, and garlic to the pan and cook for 3 minutes, stirring often.

3 Add the chili powder and cumin and cook for 1 minute. Add the tomatoes and bring to a boil. Reduce the heat to low, cover, and simmer, stirring occasionally, for 20 minutes. Add the beans, salt, and pepper, and cook for 3 minutes more.

4 Serve each portion topped with some of the cheddar cheese.

NUTRITION PER SERVING

Calories 296	Sodium 391mg
Calories from fat 89	Carbohydrate 28g
Total fat 10g	Dietary fiber 9g
Saturated fat 2.5g	Sugars 7g
Cholesterol 61mg	Protein 23g

CREAMY CHOCK-FULL-OF-CHICKEN SOUP

Heat up a chilly night with this stick-to-your-ribs creamy, chunky chicken soup. Mom will love the nutrients, and kids will love the warm goodness.

Serves: 4

Serving size: 1 cup

Preparation time: 20 minutes

Cooking time: 20 minutes

Ingredients

2 teaspoons olive oil

½ medium-size carrot, peeled and diced

½ medium-size onion, peeled and diced

1 small celery stalk, diced

¾ pound boneless, skinless chicken breasts, cut into ½-inch pieces

1½ tablespoons all-purpose flour

3 cups low-fat, reduced-sodium chicken broth, heated

1 cup 1% or fat-free milk

½ teaspoon ground sage

¼ teaspoon dried thyme

Salt and pepper to taste

1 Heat the oil in a large pot over medium-high heat. Add the carrot, onion, and celery and cook for 5 minutes, stirring occasionally. Add the chicken and cook about 3 minutes, stirring often, until no longer pink.

2 Add the flour and stir to coat the vegetables and chicken. Slowly stir in the chicken broth and milk and bring to a boil. Reduce the heat to low, stir in the sage, thyme, salt, and pepper, and simmer 5 minutes more before serving.

NUTRITION
PER SERVING

Calories 185
Calories from fat 46
Total fat 5g
    Saturated fat 1g
Cholesterol 51mg
Sodium 574mg
Carbohydrate 10g
    Dietary fiber 1g
    Sugars 5g
Protein 24g

TRIED-AND-TRUE TERIYAKI BEEF SOUP

One common complaint kids have about soup is that it's just not filling. Well, say *sayonara* to tummy-grumbling with this Asian delight. Filled with juicy beef, tender rice, and broccoli, it's a complete meal in one bowl.

Serves: 6

Serving size: 1 cup

Preparation time: 30 minutes

Cooking time: 30 minutes

Ingredients

1 teaspoon sesame oil

½ pound lean boneless sirloin steak, cut into 1-inch pieces

1 small onion, peeled and minced

1 medium-size carrot, peeled and diced

4 cups low-fat, reduced-sodium beef broth

⅓ cup long-grain rice

1 cup coarsely chopped broccoli

2 tablespoons reduced-sodium teriyaki sauce

1 Heat the oil in a large, heavy pot over medium-high heat. Add the steak and stir-fry another 3 minutes.

2 Add the broth and rice and bring to a boil. Reduce the heat to low, cover, and simmer 15 to 18 minutes until the rice is cooked.

3 Stir in the broccoli and teriyaki sauce and continue to simmer about 3 minutes, covered, until the broccoli is tender. Serve immediately.

NUTRITION PER SERVING

Calories 120	Sodium 200mg
Calories from fat 32	Carbohydrate 12g
Total fat 3.5g	Dietary fiber 1.5g
Saturated fat 1g	Sugars 2g
Cholesterol 18mg	Protein 9.5g

CHICKEN-NOT-SO-LITTLE NOODLE SOUP

If your kids love noodles in their soup but find that the thin ones always slip off the spoon, try wide noodles in this variation on a classic favorite. You can substitute leftover Thanksgiving turkey for the chicken and watch the family gobble it up.

Serves: 4

Serving size: 1 cup

Preparation time: 30 minutes

Cooking time: 40 minutes

Ingredients

2 teaspoons olive oil

1 medium-size onion, peeled and chopped

2 garlic cloves, peeled and minced

2 medium-size carrots, peeled and thinly sliced

1 pound boneless, skinless chicken breasts, cut into 1-inch cubes

2 tablespoons all-purpose flour

4 cups low-fat, reduced-sodium chicken broth

1 tablespoon finely chopped fresh thyme leaves

4 oz. dry wide egg noodles

Salt and pepper to taste

1 Heat the oil in a large pot over medium heat. Add the onion and garlic and cook, stirring occasionally, for 4 minutes.

2 Add the carrots and cook for 3 minutes more. Add the chicken and cook 5 to 6 minutes, stirring often, until lightly browned.

3 Sprinkle the flour over the mixture and stir to coat the chicken and vegetables, cooking for 1 minute. Stir in the broth and thyme, and bring to a boil. Reduce the heat to low and simmer for 20 minutes.

4 Add the noodles, increase the heat to medium-high, and cook until the noodles are tender yet firm, 7 to 8 minutes. Season to taste with salt and pepper before serving.

NUTRITION PER SERVING	
Calories 222	Sodium 180mg
Calories from fat 40	Carbohydrate 20g
Total fat 4.5g	Dietary fiber 2g
Saturated fat 1g	Sugars 2g
Cholesterol 76mg	Protein 24g

CHOW-DOWN CHICKEN-AND-PASTA SOUP

Serves: 6
Serving size: 1 cup
Preparation time: 15 minutes
Cooking time: 30 minutes

Ingredients

- 1 tablespoon olive oil
- 2 garlic cloves, peeled and chopped
- 2 medium-size carrots, peeled and thinly sliced
- 1 large onion, peeled and diced
- 1 cup cooked chicken, torn or cut into bite-size pieces
- 4 cups low-fat, reduced-sodium chicken broth
- 1 can (14 oz.) navy beans, drained and rinsed
- 1 can (14 oz.) diced Italian-style tomatoes
- 1 cup dry small pasta, such as tubetti (tiny tubes) or stelline (stars)
- 2 teaspoons dried basil
- Salt and pepper to taste
- ¼ cup Parmesan cheese

Everyone loves pasta. It's fun and nourishing, and it's also a great springboard for easy, creative, fully balanced meals. This recipe is perfect for leftover cooked chicken, but you can always substitute Perdue Shortcuts®. Hearty beans add extra protein to this true comfort food.

1 Heat the oil in a large pot over medium heat. Add the garlic, carrots, and onions, and cook about 5 minutes, stirring occasionally, until softened. Add the chicken and cook 2 minutes more. Add the broth and beans, bring to a boil, lower the heat, and simmer for 10 minutes.

2 Add the tomatoes, pasta, basil, salt, and pepper, and simmer for 10 minutes, until the pasta is cooked through. Sprinkle each serving with a little Parmesan cheese.

NUTRITION
PER SERVING

Calories 338
Calories from fat 46
Total fat 5g
  Saturated fat 1.5g
Cholesterol 16mg
Sodium 822mg
Carbohydrate 52g
  Dietary fiber 6g
  Sugars 7g
Protein 22g

Awesome Tip
Soups make a great snack, too. Even a half-portion will fill up your child with warming, nutritious ingredients. And the high volume of water will keep the hunger pangs away until dinnertime.

TOASTY TORTILLA-IN-A-CUP SOUP

One surefire way to get kids to eat their soup is by giving them the unexpected. They'll tip their sombreros to the toasty, tasty tortilla strips topping this colorful and festive soup. Add leftover shredded cooked chicken for an extra fiesta of protein and flavor.

Serves: 4

Serving size: 1 cup

Preparation time: 15 minutes

Cooking time: 50 minutes

Ingredients

2 teaspoons olive oil

1 small onion, peeled and chopped

2 garlic cloves, peeled and minced

2 teaspoons chili powder

4 cups low-fat, reduced-sodium chicken broth

1 can (14 oz.) diced tomatoes, drained

1 medium-size zucchini, trimmed and diced

1 medium-size yellow squash, trimmed and diced

1 cup frozen yellow corn, thawed

3 soft corn tortillas

⅓ cup reduced-fat shredded cheddar cheese

1 Heat the oil in a large saucepan over medium heat. Add the onion and garlic and cook for 5 minutes, stirring occasionally. Add the chili powder and sauté for 1 minute more.

2 Add the remaining ingredients, except the tortillas and cheese, and bring to a boil. Reduce the heat to low, cover, and simmer for 25 minutes.

3 Meanwhile, cut the tortillas into ½-inch strips. Place the strips on a baking sheet and bake in a preheated 350° oven for 5 to 6 minutes until the tortillas are lightly browned.

4 To serve, place some of the tortilla strips in a cup or bowl. Ladle the soup over the tortillas and top with a sprinkling of cheese.

NUTRITION
PER SERVING

Calories 180
Calories from fat 50
Total fat 6g
    Saturated fat 1.5g
Cholesterol 7mg
Sodium 790mg
Carbohydrate 26g
    Dietary fiber 4g
    Sugars 6g
Protein 10g

BLAST-OFF BAKED-AND-MASHED-POTATO SOUP

Have you ever known anyone to say no to a mashed or baked potato? This stellar soup takes off with two delicious reasons to sip your supper. It also stars tender chunks of beef in this constellation of flavors.

Serves: 6

Serving size: 1 cup

Preparation time: 20 minutes

Cooking time: 2 hours

Ingredients

2 medium-size Idaho or russet potatoes

3 slices lean bacon

2 large onions, peeled and chopped

3 garlic cloves, peeled and minced

1 bay leaf

½ pound lean round steak, cut into ½-inch cubes

3½ cups 1% milk

¼ teaspoon black pepper

1½ cups low-fat, reduced-sodium chicken broth

3 scallions, ends trimmed, thinly sliced

1 cup reduced-fat shredded cheddar cheese

1 Preheat the oven to 400°.

2 Pierce each potato with a fork and bake directly on a rack set in the middle of the oven for 1½ hours, or until fork-tender. Remove from the oven and allow to cool slightly, then scoop out the potatoes into a medium-size bowl. Mash well, using a fork or potato masher, and set aside. Discard the skins or save them for "Come and Get 'Em" Potato Skins (page 66).

3 In a medium-size skillet or frying pan, cook the bacon over medium-high heat until crisp. Transfer the strips to a paper towel to drain and allow to cool slightly, then crumble into small pieces and set aside.

4 Add the onion to the drippings in the skillet and cook about 5 minutes, stirring often, until the mixture is softened. Add the garlic and bay leaf and cook 2 more minutes. Add the steak and cook about 5 minutes, stirring often, until lightly browned. Transfer the contents of the skillet to a large saucepan, stir in the potato, milk, pepper, and broth and bring to a boil over medium-high heat. Reduce the heat to low and allow to simmer for 10 minutes.

5 To serve, ladle the soup into bowls and top with the chopped scallions, reserved bacon pieces, and cheese.

NUTRITION PER SERVING

Calories 255	Sodium 664mg
Calories from fat 58	Carbohydrate 26g
Total fat 6g	Dietary fiber 2g
Saturated fat 3g	Sugars 11g
Cholesterol 41mg	Protein 23g

NO ORDINARY BACON-AND-CHEESE SOUP

This is a rich, creamy, and cheesy soup that satisfies tummies with a lot less fat than most creamed soups. Serve with warm, crusty whole-wheat rolls.

Serves: 4

Serving size: 1 cup

Preparation time: 20 minutes

Cooking time: 30 minutes

Ingredients

2 slices lean bacon

1 small celery stalk, finely chopped

½ medium-size carrot, peeled and finely chopped

½ medium-size onion, peeled and finely chopped

¼ cup all-purpose flour

2 cups low-fat, reduced-sodium chicken broth

1 cup 1% milk

1½ cups shredded reduced-fat cheddar cheese

1 In a medium-size skillet or frying pan, cook the bacon over medium-high heat until crisp. Transfer the strips to a paper towel to drain and allow to cool slightly, then crumble into small pieces and set aside. Add the celery, carrot, and onion to the drippings in the pan and cook about 5 minutes over medium heat, stirring often, until softened.

2 Transfer the contents of the skillet to a large saucepan, stir in the flour, and cook over medium heat until bubbly but not brown. Stir in the broth and bring to a boil. Reduce the heat to low and simmer for 10 minutes.

3 Add the milk and simmer for 4 minutes more. Remove the saucepan from the heat and add the cheese in small handfuls, stirring well after each addition, until melted. To serve, ladle the soup into bowls and top with some of the reserved bacon pieces.

Awesome Tip
A mini food processor really comes in handy when finely chopped vegetables are required.

NUTRITION PER SERVING	Total fat 9g	Carbohydrate 15g	
	Saturated fat 4g	Dietary fiber 1g	
Calories 214	Cholesterol 44mg	Sugars 5g	
Calories from fat 90	Sodium 705mg	Protein 18g	

CREAMY CARROT TOP-TO-BOTTOM SOUP

Peter Rabbit wouldn't be able to resist the garden of flavors in this smooth carrot soup. Cottontails will come hopping for more of this nutritious and creamy delight. With the natural sweetness of carrots and a hint of cinnamon, this soup may have your kids asking for a second helping instead of dessert.

Serves: 4

Serving size: 1 cup

Preparation time: 20 minutes

Cooking time: 45 minutes

Ingredients

2 teaspoons olive oil

1 small onion, peeled and finely chopped

1 garlic clove, peeled and minced

3 large carrots, peeled and thinly sliced

2 cups low-fat, reduced-sodium chicken broth

1 cup 1% milk

½ teaspoon ground cinnamon

Salt and pepper to taste

1 Heat the oil in a large saucepan over medium heat. Add the onion and garlic and cook 2 to 3 minutes, stirring often, until mixture softens. Add the carrots and sauté for two more 2 minutes. Add the broth and bring to a boil. Reduce the heat to low and cook at a simmer for about 8 minutes until the carrots are fork-tender.

2 Transfer the mixture to a food processor or blender and purée until smooth. Return to saucepan, add the milk, cinnamon, salt, and pepper, stir well to combine, and cook at a low simmer for 3 to 4 minutes. Serve immediately.

NUTRITION PER SERVING

Calories 100
Calories from fat 34
Total fat 4g
    Saturated fat 1g
Cholesterol 3mg
Sodium 176mg
Carbohydrate 13g
    Dietary fiber 2g
    Sugars 7g
Protein 5g

MORE MINESTRONE SOUP, PLEASE

There may be no better way for kids to eat their veggies than in good old minestrone. The pasta helps, of course, but kids will holler anyway for this hearty soup packed with flavor. Every spoonful is filled with nutritional goodness and is sure to satisfy the grumbling of hungry tummies.

Serves: 6

Serving size: 1 cup

Preparation time: 15 minutes

Cooking time: 30 minutes

Ingredients

2 teaspoons olive oil

½ medium-size onion, peeled and diced

2 garlic cloves, peeled and minced

1 medium-size carrot, peeled and diced

1 medium-size celery stalk, trimmed and diced

1 small zucchini, trimmed and diced

5 cups low-fat, reduced-sodium chicken broth

1 can (14 oz.) diced tomatoes, drained

½ cup dry elbow macaroni

1 cup kidney beans, drained and rinsed

½ teaspoon dried basil

Salt and pepper to taste

1 Heat the oil in a large saucepan over medium-high heat. Add the onion, garlic, carrot, celery, and zucchini and cook about 5 minutes, stirring occasionally, until softened.

2 Stir in the broth and tomatoes and bring to a boil. Reduce the heat to low and simmer for 5 minutes.

3 Increase the heat to medium-high, add the macaroni, and cook at a medium simmer for about 7 minutes, stirring occasionally, until tender. Stir in the beans, basil, salt, and pepper and cook 3 minutes more. Serve immediately.

Awesome Tip

Even in summer months, it pays to prepare soup for later use. Most soups freeze well, so start preparing soup for fall and winter in August. Place in freezer in sealable plastic bags or plastic containers. Soup will be ready in a jiffy on a cold night.

NUTRITION PER SERVING
Calories 147
Calories from fat 28

Total fat 3g
   Saturated fat .5g
Cholesterol 0mg
Sodium 314mg

Carbohydrate 23g
Dietary fiber 5g
Sugars 5g
Protein 9g

CRAZY-FOR-CORN SOUP

Corn lovers unite! We've *corn*ered the market with this thick and creamy soup that's packed with protein and has little of the usual fat. It can be served up in no time, and you'd be *crazy* not to love it.

Serves: 4
Serving size: 1 cup
Preparation time: 15 minutes
Cooking time: 25 minutes

Ingredients

1 tablespoon olive oil

1 medium-size onion, peeled and diced

1 medium-size red potato, peeled and cut into ½-inch dice

1 cup low-fat, reduced-sodium chicken broth

2 cups frozen corn kernels, thawed

2 cups evaporated skim milk

Salt and pepper to taste

Dash of paprika

1 cup diced cooked turkey or chicken

1 tablespoon cornstarch

¼ cup cold water

1. Heat the oil in a large, heavy saucepan over medium heat. Add the onion and cook about 5 minutes, stirring occasionally, until softened. Stir in the broth, add the diced potato, and cook about 5 minutes at a low simmer until the potatoes are almost fork-tender.

2. Add the corn, milk, salt, pepper, and paprika and stir to combine. Bring to a simmer over medium heat and cook for 10 minutes, stirring occasionally. Stir in the diced turkey or chicken and continue to cook on low for 5 more minutes.

3. In a small mixing bowl, dissolve the cornstarch in the water and stir into the soup. Allow to cook about 2 minutes at a low simmer, stirring often, until thickened. Taste for the addition of salt and serve immediately.

NUTRITION PER SERVING		
Calories 147	Total fat 3g	Carbohydrate 23g
Calories from fat 28	Saturated fat .5g	Dietary fiber 5g
	Cholesterol 0mg	Sugars 5g
	Sodium 314mg	Protein 9g

HOLIDAY SWEET-POTATO-AND-APPLE SOUP

This "sweet" potato soup is also great as a make-ahead appetizer for Thanksgiving or any occasion you think is special. Prepare up to two days ahead, then reheat on the stove and serve when it's time to celebrate.

Serves: 6

Serving size: ½ cup

Preparation time: 15 minutes

Cooking time: 1 hour

Ingredients

2 teaspoons olive oil

1 small onion, peeled and finely chopped

1 pound (about 2 medium-size) sweet potatoes, peeled and cut into 1½-inch cubes

1 teaspoon granulated sugar

1 McIntosh apple, peeled, cored, and diced

½ teaspoon dried thyme

Salt and pepper to taste

3 cups low-fat, reduced-sodium chicken broth

1 Heat the oil in a large saucepan over medium heat. Add the onion and cook about 2 minutes, stirring often, until softened. Add the remaining ingredients except the broth, stir well, and continue to cook over medium heat for about 5 minutes, stirring occasionally.

2 Add the broth, increase the heat to medium-high, and bring to a boil. Reduce the heat to low, cover, and simmer for about 30 minutes until the potatoes are very tender.

3 Transfer the mixture to a food processor or blender and purée until smooth. Serve immediately or refrigerate.

Awesome Tip: For an even creamier version stir in ½ cup heated fat-free half-and-half before serving.

NUTRITION PER SERVING

Calories 147	Sodium 314mg
Calories from fat 28	Carbohydrate 23g
Total fat 3g	Dietary fiber 5g
Saturated fat .5g	Sugars 5g
Cholesterol 0mg	Protein 9g

Smoothies
and Other Drinks

RAZZAMATAZZ
RASPBERRY COOLER

HOMEMADE SWEET-
AND-SASSY LEMONADE

FANTASTIC FIZZY
STRAWBERRY SHAKE

SMOOTHIES AND OTHER DRINKS

Thanks to the popularity of healthy smoothies and other assorted drinks, children can now almost drink their way to health. It's an approach that's quick and portable. Instead of sugary sodas and pure fruit juices (which also contain a lot of sugar), the smoothie recipes here contain far fewer simple carbohydrates. And if your child is picky about fruits, what better way to disguise them than in a cool smoothie?

If your child needs extra nutrition, a blender drink is the perfect vehicle for adding things like protein powder, nonfat dry milk powder, wheat germ, low-fat/low-sugar peanut butter, and more. On their own, these ingredients may not pass the taste test, but when they're blended together, your child can get an extra boost of nutrition while tasting only the predominant ingredients such as milk and fruit.

For best results with blender drinks, make sure your blender is powerful enough to handle pieces of ice and that the power is sufficient to ensure a very smooth drink. Most of the smoothies in this chapter can even be prepared up to half an hour before serving, giving your child a chance to get ready for school or to rest a bit after playing.

To make smoothies even more fun, pour them into tall glasses and have your child sip from a fun straw. Half the battle is won when food can be presented in an inviting way that makes children feel just like everyone else.

Other hot and cold drinks that keep fat, sugar, and calories low are great refreshments as well. You'll find a terrific selection here to suit every taste!

HOMEMADE SWEET-AND-SASSY LEMONADE

It's summertime and the lemons are easy – especially in this lemony drink, made with Splenda to provide the sweetness without the sugar content.

Serves: 8

Serving size: ½ cup

Preparation time: 15 minutes

Ingredients

Juice of 3 lemons

½ cup Splenda

1 cup hot water

3 cups cold water

Ice cubes

Mint leaves (optional)

1 In a large pitcher, combine the lemon juice, Splenda, and hot water. Stir until the Splenda is dissolved, add the cold water and ice cubes, and stir well. Cover and refrigerate for at least half an hour before serving. Garnish with mint leaves, if desired.

NUTRITION PER SERVING

Calories 12	Carbohydrate 3.5g
Total fat 0	Dietary fiber .5g
Cholesterol 0	Sugars .5g
Sodium 5mg	Protein 0

WET-AND-WILD WATERMELON DRINK

Listening to kids slurping on watermelon slices makes you think they'd like to drink it as well as eat it. Well, here's the solution. Combine watermelon and ice cream to provide a cool, creamy, and refreshing drink in the summertime.

Serves: 2

Serving size: 1 cup

Preparation time: 15 minutes

Ingredients

1 cup watermelon chunks, seeds removed

¼ cup low-sugar grape juice

½ cup light vanilla ice cream

½ cup crushed ice

RAZZAMATAZZ RASPBERRY COOLER

Jazz up a hot day with this sweet berry drink. Low in sugar and high in calcium, this cool drink is really *razz*.

Serves: 2

Serving size: ½ cup

Preparation time: 5 minutes

Ingredients

1 cup fresh raspberries

½ cup light vanilla ice cream

½ cup very cold 1% or
    fat-free milk

Fresh raspberries for garnish

1 Combine all the ingredients in a blender and purée until smooth. Serve immediately, garnished with a few raspberries.

NUTRITION PER SERVING

Calories 100	Sodium 175mg
Calories from fat 28g	Carbohydrate 13g
Total fat 4g	Dietary fiber 2g
Saturated fat 1g	Sugars 7g
Cholesterol 3mg	Protein 5g

1 Place the watermelon, grape juice, and ice cream in a blender. Purée until smooth. To serve, divide the ice between two glasses and pour the watermelon mixture over each.

NUTRITION PER SERVING

Calories 92

Calories from fat 23

Total fat 2.5g

   Saturated fat 1g

Cholesterol 9mg

Sodium 34mg

Carbohydrate 17g

   Dietary fiber .5g

   Sugars 11.5g

Protein 2g

FANTASTIC FIZZY STRAWBERRY SHAKE

The season for summer strawberries is all too short, so we always try to make the most of it by buying them up when they appear. If, however, you find you have more berries than you can handle, this lightly sweet and fruity, fizzy fun-in-a-glass is the answer. When fresh berries are out of season, feel free to use frozen strawberries without added sugar.

Serves: 6

Serving size: ½ cup

Preparation time: 5 minutes

Ingredients

1 cup fresh strawberries, washed and hulled

½ cup fat-free milk

12 oz. plain seltzer water or club soda

2 tablespoons Splenda

1 Combine all ingredients in a blender and purée until smooth. Pour into glasses and serve immediately.

NUTRITION PER SERVING

Calories 23	Carbohydrate 5g
Total fat 0	Dietary fiber 1g
Cholesterol 0	Sugars 2.5g
Sodium 22mg	Protein 1g

COSMIC CRANBERRY-BANANA COOLER

Serves: 4

Serving size: ½ cup

Preparation time: 5 minutes

Ingredients

1 banana, peeled and cut into 1-inch chunks, frozen

1 cup low-calorie cranberry juice

1 cup plain seltzer water

2 tablespoons Splenda

Ice cubes

Sometimes a banana just tastes better when it's icy cold and frozen, and this cranberry-banana combo is simply stellar. A glass of this cosmic drink is the rocket fuel that will keep your child soaring on a hot day.

1 Combine the first four ingredients in a blender and add enough ice to fill half the blender pitcher. Purée until smooth and serve immediately.

NUTRITION PER SERVING

Calories 42	Carbohydrate 11g
Total fat 0	Dietary fiber 1g
Cholesterol 0	Sugars 8g
Sodium 14mg	Protein 0g

MARVELOUS MANGO LASSI

The lassi, invented in India, is a superhealthy version of a milk-shake. It's light and frothy fun in a glass. Try using the traditional ingredient of honey rather than Splenda to sweeten if carbs can be spared. Mango and yogurt never tasted so good!

1 Combine all ingredients in a blender and purée until smooth. Serve immediately.

NUTRITION PER SERVING

Calories 37	Carbohydrate 7.5g
Total fat 0	Dietary fiber 1g
Cholesterol 1mg	Sugars 4g
Sodium 36mg	Protein 3g

Serves: 4

Serving size: 1 cup

Preparation time: 15 minutes

Ingredients

1 soft mango, peeled and cut into cubes, the large seed discarded

1 cup fat-free plain yogurt

2 tablespoons Splenda or honey

1½ cups ice cubes

SUPER-SIPPY SUMMER-SUN TEA

Why brew tea on a hot day when tea will brew itself? A big jar of refreshing sun tea provides a continuous supply of everyone's favorite summertime treat. Flavor with mint leaves, sliced oranges, sliced lemons, or cinnamon sticks.

Serves: 16

Serving size: 1 cup

Preparation time: 5 to 6 hours

Ingredients

4 caffeine-free tea bags

1 gallon water

¼ to ½ cup Splenda, to taste

Flavoring (see above)

1 Cut off the strings and tags from the tea bags and place them in a gallon-size pitcher or sun-tea jar fitted with a lid. Add the water, cover, and set in the sun for 4 hours.

2 Remove the tea bags, stir in the Splenda and desired flavoring, and place in the refrigerator to chill for 1 to 2 hours before serving.

NUTRITION PER SERVING

Calories 3	Carbohydrate 1g
Total fat 0	Dietary fiber 0
Cholesterol 0	Sugars 0
Sodium 5mg	Protein 0

PEACHY-KEEN "HOLD THE FUZZ" FRAPPÉ

Okay, a real frappé is more like a sherbet, but no one will quibble over the taste of this peachy treat. It's best during peach season, but in a pinch you can also use canned or frozen peaches.

Serves: 8

Serving size: ½ cup

Preparation time: 10 minutes

Ingredients

1 cup fresh diced peaches, skin removed

1 cup fat-free milk

¼ cup nonfat peach yogurt

½ cup Splenda

2 cups ice cubes

1 Combine all ingredients in a blender and purée until smooth. Serve immediately.

NUTRITION PER SERVING

Calories 67

Total fat 0

Cholesterol 2mg

Sodium 35mg

Carbohydrate 13g

Dietary fiber 1g

Sugars

Protein 2.5g

Awesome Tip

For variety and added protein, use soy milk in place of cow's milk in any smoothie. Most soy milks are calcium-fortified, just as regular milk is, and can be very useful for children with lactose intolerance. Just be sure to count the additional fat and carbs that they may contribute.

FAB BLUEBERRY **BLAST**

Fresh or frozen blueberries can be used to create this fab smoothie. Blasting with fruity flavor, it's berry, berry good!

Serves: 6

Serving size: ½ cup

Preparation time: 10 minutes

Ingredients

1 cup fat-free blueberry-flavored yogurt

½ cup fresh blueberries, washed and stems removed

1 cup of fat-free milk

1 tablespoon Splenda

1 ½ cup ice cubes

NUTRITION PER SERVING

Calories 47	Carbohydrate 8g
Total fat 0	Dietary fiber .5g
Cholesterol 2mg	Sugars 6g
Sodium 45mg	Protein 3g

1 Combine all ingredients in a blender and purée until smooth. Serve immediately.

COOL MINTY HOT COCOA

It may be cold outside, but how about something "cool" to keep you warm? This variation on conventional cocoa tastes just like a Thin Mint Girl Scout Cookie.

Serves: 4

Serving size: ½ cup

Preparation time: 5 minutes

Cooking time: 5 minutes

Ingredients

2 teaspoons unsweetened cocoa powder

2 tablespoons Splenda

5 sugar-free striped, round peppermint candies, finely crushed

2 cups 1% or fat-free milk

1 In a small saucepan over medium heat, whisk together the cocoa, Splenda, crushed candies, and ½ cup of milk. Cook, whisking constantly, until the mixture comes just to a boil and the cocoa and candies are melted. Stir in the remaining milk and heat through without boiling. Serve immediately.

NUTRITION PER SERVING

Calories 68	Sodium 73mg
Calories from fat 4	Carbohydrate 11g
Total fat .5g	Dietary fiber .5g
Saturated fat 0g	Sugars 5g
Cholesterol 3mg	Protein 5g

GET YOUR RED-HOT APPLE CIDER

When apple season is over, hot-apple-cider season is just beginning, and there's nothing like a candy-apple drink for fall. It will warm your child from the nose down to the toes.

Serves: 4

Serving size: ½ cup

Preparation time: 10 minutes

Cooking time: 7 minutes

Ingredients

1 cup "no sugar added" apple juice

1 cup water

1 tablespoon cinnamon-red-hot candies

5 whole cloves

1 In a small saucepan over medium heat, combine all the ingredients and allow to simmer for 5 minutes. Remove the red-hot candies and cloves with a slotted spoon and discard. Pour the cider into mugs and serve immediately.

NUTRITION PER SERVING

Calories 73	Carbohydrate 18g
Total fat 0	Dietary fiber 1g
Cholesterol 0	Sugars 14g
Sodium 7mg	Protein 0

Awesome Tip: Use unfiltered apple juice to provide some extra fiber.

The Lunchbox

LUNCH TIME!

"I'll trade you a ham sandwich for your peanut-butter sandwich."

"Throw in two cookies, and you've got a deal!"

Children can be cunning deal-makers when it comes to their lunches. And all too often, what's sent with them to school doesn't end up in their stomachs. Worse yet, many school lunch programs today provide large proportions of high-fat, high-sugar foods.

You know that lunch is important for your child. The question is how to make it appealing enough that it won't be traded away or replaced with something from the school cafeteria.

If you make the midday meal fun and simple, your child will eventually look forward to discovering what's hidden inside the lunchbox. Imagine the delight at finding Tangy Tuna Fish Sandwiches (page 51) in the shape of fish, or a pasta salad instead of a sandwich. Your child will also get a kick out of rolling ingredients inside a tortilla while helping you prepare school lunches and will have even more fun eating it.

Keep in mind that your child is going to be active after lunch right up until dinnertime so it's very important that blood-sugar levels remain stable throughout after-school activities. A good solid lunch can make the difference in whether your child succeeds in the classroom, out on the field, and with all the other activities that occupy busy children today. With these creative "out-of-the-box" ideas, lunchtime will surely become less of a worry for you and more of a delight for your child.

PARTY-TIME PPB&J SANDWICHES

The addition of pear (accounting for the extra "P" in PPB&J) adds an extra burst of flavor to these peanut butter and jelly sandwiches.

Serves: 4

Serving size: ½ sandwich

Preparation time: 10 minutes

Ingredients

4 thin slices whole-wheat raisin bread

3 tablespoons reduced-fat peanut butter

3 tablespoons sugar-free jelly (flavor of choice)

½ cup diced pear, unpeeled

1 Spread 2 slices of bread with the peanut butter and jam. Distribute the pear on top. Finish each sandwich with the remaining slice of bread and cut in half to serve.

NUTRITION PER SERVING
Calories 154
Calories from fat 50
Total fat 6g
　Saturated fat 1g
Cholesterol 0
Sodium 161mg
Carbohydrate 25g
　Dietary fiber 2.5g
　Sugars 5g
Protein 5g

POSITIVELY PEANUTTY NOODLES

Sometimes the only thing better than noodles is more noodles! Here's a light variation on a Chinese favorite, and it's an excellent accompaniment to a favorite Asian dish, such as Very Teriyaki Shrimp (page 106).

Serves: 2

Serving size: 1 cup

Preparation time: 5 minutes

Cooking time: 10-12 minutes

Ingredients

3 oz. Chinese noodles, cooked according to package directions, drained, and rinsed under cold water

¼ cup reduced-fat, low-sodium chicken broth

2 tablespoons smooth peanut butter

2 teaspoons reduced-sodium soy sauce

1 teaspoon rice vinegar

½ teaspoon ground ginger

1 In a medium-size microwave-safe bowl, whisk together all ingredients except the noodles. Microwave on high for 30 seconds. Whisk again until smooth.

2 Add the cooked noodles to the peanut-butter mixture and toss well to coat. Serve immediately or cover and refrigerate for up to two days.

NUTRITION PER SERVING

Calories 122
Calories from fat 36
Total fat 4g
    Saturated fat 1g
Cholesterol 0
Sodium 155mg
Carbohydrate 17g
    Dietary fiber 1g
    Sugars 1g
Protein 3g

CHUNKY CHICKEN-AND-GRAPE-SALAD WRAPS

Serves: 2

Serving size: 1 tortilla

Preparation time: 5 minutes

Ingredients

For the chicken salad:

1 cup cooked chicken breast, diced

1 small celery stalk, trimmed and diced

¼ cup halved red seedless grapes

1 scallion, trimmed and finely chopped

2 tablespoons sliced almonds, toasted

¼ cup reduced-fat mayonnaise

Juice of half a lemon

Salt and pepper to taste

---

2 lettuce leaves, romaine or Bibb

2 whole-wheat flour tortillas (6 inches each)

Wraps are all the rage, and no wonder. These handy chicken-salad parcels are great for a picnic, lunch, after-school snack, or light summer dinner. This fruity version is filled with healthful, crunchy ingredients. It's a wrap.

1 In a medium-size bowl, combine the chicken, celery, grapes, scallions, and almonds.

2 In a small mixing bowl, whisk together the remaining salad ingredients. Gently fold into the chicken mixture until well combined.

3 Place one lettuce leaf on each tortilla. Divide the chicken salad and spread it over the top half of each lettuce leaf. Fold the bottom of the tortilla, then roll it to close. Serve immediately or wrap in plastic and refrigerate.

NUTRITION PER SERVING

Calories 367

Calories from fat 95

Total fat 8g

    Saturated fat 2g

Cholesterol 57mg

Sodium 438mg

Carbohydrate 34g

    Dietary fiber 3g

    Sugars 6g

Protein 24g

TANGY TUNA FISH "CUT-OUT" SANDWICHES

Even for children who as a rule don't enjoy fish, tuna fish makes a sandwich filling that's tasty, healthful, and easy to prepare. To add appeal and turn lunch-making into a creative opportunity, use a variety of cookie-cutters so that family members can choose their own sandwich shapes.

Serves: 4

Serving size: 1 sandwich

Preparation time: 15 minutes

Ingredients

For the tuna salad:

1 can (3 oz.) solid white tuna in water, drained

2 tablespoons minced celery

1 tablespoon minced onion

¼ cup reduced-fat mayonnaise

2 tablespoons reduced-fat ranch dressing

8 thin slices whole-grain bread

RECIPE ADAPTED FROM
Kid Favorites Made Healthy,
Better Homes and Gardens Books,
Meredith Corporation, 2003.

1 In a small mixing bowl, combine all the ingredients for the tuna salad, stirring with a fork to break up the tuna pieces. Refrigerate until ready to use.

2 Using cookie-cutters, cut the bread slices into fish or other shapes. Reserve crusts for another use.

3 Spread the tuna salad evenly on half the bread shapes and top with the matching bread shapes. Serve immediately or wrap in plastic and refrigerate for a packed lunch.

Awesome Tip: Make lunch more inviting. Pack your child's lunch in a colorful lunch sack rather than a brown paper bag and purchase colorful insulated containers for perishable items.

NUTRITION PER SERVING

Calories 189
Calories from fat 44
Total fat 5g
    Saturated fat 1g
Cholesterol 10mg

Sodium 439mg
Carbohydrate 32g
    Dietary fiber 10g
    Sugars 3g
Protein 9g

YOU'RE-MAKIN'-ME-DIZZY SPIRAL SANDWICH

These multicolored roll-ups will bring out the artist in anyone. Pick your favorite cheese to go with the roast beef in this wrap sandwich. Serve it as a snack by cutting the wrap into slices.

Serves: 4

Serving size: ½ roll

Preparation time: 10 minutes

Ingredients

2 teaspoons honey mustard

2 flour tortillas (6 inches each)

2 oz. reduced-fat Swiss, provolone, or cheddar cheese, shredded

2 oz. lean roast beef

¼ cup shredded carrot

1 tablespoon raisins

1 Spread the mustard evenly over the tortillas.

2 Place the cheese, roast beef, carrots, and raisins on each tortilla, roll tightly, and slice or cut in half to serve.

NUTRITION PER SERVING

Calories 138
Calories from fat 52
Total fat 6g
   Saturated fat 2.5g

Cholesterol 21mg
Sodium 265mg
Carbohydrate 13g
   Dietary fiber .5g
   Sugars 3.5g

Protein 9g

Awesome Tip: Lunch is an extremely important part of your child's meal plan. Make sure it contains a portion of protein, a portion of carbohydrate, and a small amount of fat. The protein will help your child to concentrate on schoolwork, the carbohydrate will provide energy, and the small amount of fat will help your child keep from becoming too hungry. For example, 3 ounces of turkey with 1 ounce of cheese in a whole-wheat pita, with a side of raw vegetables, a low-fat dip of ranch dressing, and a small piece of fruit will meet these requirements.

54

TASTY TORTELLINI-TO-GO SALAD

Back to school means books – and potlucks. This pasta-lover's pleasure is packed with flavor and is just perfect for potlucks, picnics, and packed lunches. Served warm or cold, it's also terrific as a side dish when you're grilling.

Serves: 8

Serving size: ½ cup

Preparation time: 20 minutes

Cooking time: 10 minutes

Ingredients

9 oz. reduced-fat cheese tortellini

1 cup broccoli florets

1 small carrot, peeled and sliced

1 medium-size ripe tomato, seeded and diced

2 scallions, trimmed and finely sliced

¼ cup reduced-fat French dressing

¼ cup reduced-fat cheddar cheese, diced

Salt and pepper to taste

1 Bring a medium-size pot of water to a boil. Cook the tortellini according to package directions, and during the final 3 minutes add the broccoli and carrots. Drain through a colander, rinse under cold water, then set aside to drain well.

2 In a large mixing bowl combine the cooked tortellini, broccoli, and carrots with the tomato, scallions, and French dressing. Toss gently to coat, then stir in the cheese. Season with salt and pepper to taste, and serve immediately or refrigerate.

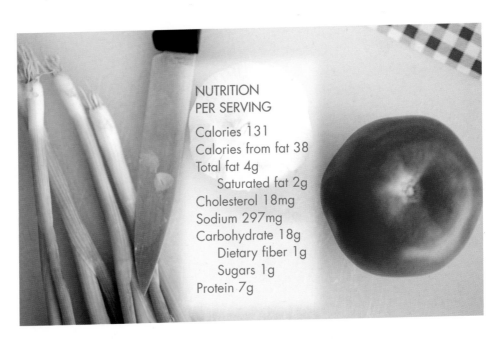

NUTRITION
PER SERVING

Calories 131
Calories from fat 38
Total fat 4g
   Saturated fat 2g
Cholesterol 18mg
Sodium 297mg
Carbohydrate 18g
   Dietary fiber 1g
   Sugars 1g
Protein 7g

TURKEY-WALDORF PITA POCKET

You won't need top hat and tails or an evening gown for this elegant affair. We have taken the rich Waldorf salad and modestly trimmed it to include a mixture of fruit and turkey breast, along with almonds for a special crunch.

Serves: 8

Serving size: ½ pocket

Preparation time: 20 minutes

Ingredients

For the turkey salad:

1 cup cooked turkey breast, diced

½ medium-size apple, peeled, cored, and diced

1 medium-size celery stalk, trimmed and diced

2 tablespoons raisins

2 tablespoons sliced almonds, toasted

3 tablespoons reduced-fat sour cream

1 tablespoon reduced-fat mayonnaise

1 teaspoon lemon juice

Salt and pepper to taste

2 small whole-wheat pita breads, cut in half to form pockets

1 In a medium-size mixing bowl, combine the turkey, apple, celery, raisins, and almonds.

2 In a small mixing bowl, whisk together the remaining salad ingredients. Gently fold them into the turkey mixture until well combined.

3 Spoon the salad into the four pita pockets and serve immediately or wrap in plastic and refrigerate for a packed lunch.

NUTRITION
PER SERVING

Calories 183
Calories from fat 38
Total fat 4g
        Saturated fat 1g
Cholesterol 51mg
Sodium 228mg
Carbohydrate 17g
        Dietary fiber 2g
        Sugars 6g
Protein 20g

Awesome Tip: To toast a small amount of nuts, place in a dry skillet and cook over medium-high heat for about 1 or 2 minutes, shaking often.

FABULOUS FRUITY BAGEL SANDWICH

Bagels aren't just for breakfast. A little creative thinking can turn a bagel into lunch or an after-school treat. Just add fruit to make it a well-balanced and tasty meal.

Serves: 4

Serving size: 1 bagel

Preparation time: 10 minutes

Ingredients

3 oz. nonfat cream cheese

½ teaspoon ground cinnamon

1 teaspoon lemon juice

4 small whole-wheat bagels, split

1 small banana, peeled and sliced

½ medium-size apple, cored and thinly sliced

1 In a small bowl, stir together the cream cheese, cinnamon, and lemon juice. Divide and spread the mixture on four of the bagel halves. Add the fruit slices and top with the remaining halves. Serve immediately.

NUTRITION PER SERVING

Calories 210
Calories from fat 12
Total fat 1g
        Saturated fat .5g
Cholesterol 2mg
Sodium 451mg
Carbohydrate 42g
        Dietary fiber 7g
        Sugars 7g
Protein 11g

After-School Snacks

AFTER-SCHOOL SNACKS

Small, frequent meals work well for most children, whether they have diabetes or not. Little stomachs coupled with high energy means that most children are ready to eat at least every three or four hours when they're awake. Snacks can take on special importance in diabetes situations and can be your secret weapon for avoiding rigid meal plans while still keeping blood sugar under control.

Although there are some good ones on the market today, prepackaged snacks almost always have too much of something: sugar, carbohydrates, fat, chemicals. So why not have some goodies ready when your child is hungry? And teaching children to prepare their own snacks is a great way to introduce them to the entire concept of cooking.

The following fun snacks are easy to prepare and use common ingredients. Not only will they help your child make it through to dinner, they have all the qualities of a super-satisfying treat.

CRISPY PARMESAN CHIPS

Instead of using either high-fat chips or the bland-tasting low-fat ones, why not help your kids make their own? These chips require no dip, since the flavor is baked in. Bet you can't eat just one.

Serves: 6

Serving size: 10 chips

Preparation time: 30 minutes

Cooking time: 8 to 10 minutes

Ingredients

30 square wonton wrappers

Cooking spray

Salt (optional)

2 tablespoons olive oil

1 garlic clove, peeled and minced

½ teaspoon dried basil

¼ cup grated Parmesan cheese

1 Preheat the oven to 350°. Coat a large baking sheet with cooking spray.

2 Using a sharp knife, cut the wonton wrappers in half diagonally to form 60 triangles. Arrange as many of the triangles as will fit on the prepared baking sheet in a single layer. If you wish, sprinkle with a dash of salt.

3 In a small mixing bowl, whisk together the olive oil, garlic, and basil, and lightly brush the top of each wonton triangle with the mixture. Sprinkle some of the cheese on top, and bake until golden-brown, 8 to 10 minutes.

4 Transfer the chips to a wire rack to cool completely. Repeat with the remaining wonton triangles. Store any uneaten chips in an airtight plastic bag or container.

NUTRITION PER SERVING

Calories 174
Calories from fat 56
Total fat 6g
  Saturated fat 1g
Cholesterol 6mg

Sodium 303mg
Carbohydrate 23g
  Dietary fiber 1g
  Sugars 0
Protein 5g

SOUTH SEAS TROPICAL FRUIT KEBABS

Here's a fun way to enjoy a variety of fruits. Kids love dips, and this vanilla yogurt spiked with orange and cinnamon will give them a reason to eat more fruit.

Serves: 4

Serving size: 1 kebab

Preparation time: 35 minutes

Ingredients

½ cup each fresh cubed cantaloupe, honeydew, pineapple, and halved strawberries

1 small banana, peeled and cut into 1-inch pieces

3 tablespoons orange juice

1 tablespoon lime juice

For the dip:

½ cup low-fat creamy vanilla yogurt

1 tablespoon orange juice concentrate, thawed

½ teaspoon cinnamon

1 Alternately thread the fruit pieces on 4 skewers and place in a shallow baking dish. Stir together the orange and lime juices and pour evenly over the fruit. Cover and refrigerate for 30 minutes.

2 Meanwhile, in a small mixing bowl, whisk together the dip ingredients and refrigerate until ready to serve.

3 Transfer the dip to a small bowl, place in the center of a medium-size platter, and arrange the kebabs decoratively. Serve immediately.

NUTRITION
PER SERVING

Calories 119
Calories from fat 9
Total fat 1g
    Saturated fat .5g
Cholesterol 3mg
Sodium 46mg
Carbohydrate 26g
    Dietary fiber 2g
    Sugars 20g
Protein 4g

SPICY, FINGER-LICKIN' FRIED CHICKEN STRIPS WITH BLUE CHEESE DIP

Your kids will, indeed, lick their fingers when they eat these chicken tenders. As a quick pick-me-up protein snack, these chicken strips burst with flavors that kids love.

Ingredients

For the dip:

½ cup nonfat mayonnaise

1 tablespoon red wine vinegar

1 small garlic clove, peeled and minced

¼ cup crumbled blue cheese

¼ teaspoon salt

Freshly ground black pepper

For the chicken:

1 pound chicken tenderloins, trimmed

½ cup low-fat buttermilk

Dash of Tabasco sauce

½ cup all-purpose flour

½ teaspoon salt

½ teaspoon paprika

¼ teaspoon freshly ground black pepper

Dash of ground red pepper

1½ tablespoons canola oil

Serves: 6

Serving size: 1 strip

Preparation time: 30 minutes

Cooking time: 20 minutes

1 In a small mixing bowl, stir together the dip ingredients, cover, and set in the refrigerator until ready to serve.

2 In a shallow bowl, combine the buttermilk and Tabasco®. In another shallow bowl combine the flour, salt, paprika, black pepper, and ground red pepper. Moisten the tenderloins in the buttermilk mixture, then dredge each one in the flour mixture, shaking off any excess. Set aside on a clean plate.

3 Heat the oil in a heavy nonstick skillet over medium-high heat. Add the tenders and cook about 3 minutes per side until crispy and golden. Remove and drain on paper towels.

4 To serve, transfer the dip to a small bowl and place in the center of a platter, arranging the chicken around it.

NUTRITION
PER SERVING

Calories 169
Calories from fat 52
Total fat 6g
    Saturated fat 1.5g
Cholesterol 48mg
Sodium 560mg
Carbohydrate 10g
    Dietary fiber 1g
    Sugars 3g
Protein 18g

MEXICAN-HAY-RIDE ROLL-UPS

Serves: 4

Serving size: 2 pieces

Preparation time: 10 minutes

There's no end to what you can do with these roll-ups. Add sliced lean turkey or roast beef for a more substantial snack or even a light lunch.

1 In a small mixing bowl, blend the cream cheese and cheddar cheese. Stir in the salsa, scallions, and chili powder. Spread the mixture evenly on each tortilla and roll-up.

2 To serve, cut each tortilla into 4 equal pieces.

Ingredients

2 tablespoons reduced-fat cream cheese, softened

¼ cup shredded reduced-fat cheddar cheese

¼ cup mild or spicy salsa

1 scallion, trimmed and finely sliced

¼ teaspoon chili powder

2 whole-wheat tortillas (6 inches each)

NUTRITION
PER SERVING

Calories 80
Calories from fat 28
Total fat 3g
    Saturated fat 2g
Cholesterol 9mg
Sodium 267mg
Carbohydrate 12g
    Dietary fiber 1g
    Sugars 1g
Protein 4g

"COME AND GET 'EM" POTATO SKINS

For every person who throws away a vitamin-rich potato skin, there's someone else who would fight for it. Bake extra potatoes for dinner the night before and you'll have a fun snack for the kids the next day when they arrive home hungry from school.

NUTRITION PER SERVING

Calories 100
Calories from fat 14
Total fat 2g
  Saturated fat 1g
Cholesterol 8mg

Sodium 77mg
Carbohydrate 18g
  Dietary fiber 2g
  Sugars 2g
Protein 5g

Serves: 8

Serving size: 1 potato skin

Preparation time: 45 minutes

Cooking time: 15 minutes

Ingredients

4 small Idaho or russet potatoes

½ cup shredded reduced-fat cheddar cheese

½ cup nonfat sour cream

2 scallions, trimmed and finely sliced

1 Preheat the oven to 400°.

2 Scrub the potatoes well and pierce each one with a fork. Bake the potatoes about 45 minutes until fork-tender, and set aside to cool.

3 Cut the potatoes in half lengthwise and scoop out most of the inside, leaving a ½-inch-thick shell. Place the potatoes skin side down on a baking sheet and sprinkle the cheese on top. Bake about 15 minutes until the potatoes are well heated throughout and the cheese is bubbly.

4 To serve, transfer to a serving platter, top each potato with a dollop of sour cream, and finish with a sprinkling of scallions.

CINNAMON-BANANA "MAY I HAVE MORE?" CAKE

Serves: 8

Serving size: 1 slice

Preparation time: 15 minutes

Cooking time: 25 minutes

Ingredients

Cooking spray

1 cup all-purpose flour

½ cup whole-wheat flour

¾ cup Splenda

2 teaspoons baking powder

1 teaspoon baking soda

2 teaspoons ground cinnamon

½ teaspoon salt

1 cup low-fat vanilla yogurt

2 medium-size ripe bananas, peeled and mashed

2 tablespoons canola oil

1 large egg, beaten

¼ cup 1% or skim milk

1 teaspoon vanilla extract

Kids love eating cakes and baking them, too! This moist, easy-to-make banana cake is perfect for an afternoon snack.

1 Preheat the oven to 400°. Coat a square 8 x 8-inch baking pan with cooking spray.

2 In a large mixing bowl, whisk together the flours, Splenda, baking powder, baking soda, cinnamon, and salt. In a medium-size mixing bowl, combine the yogurt, bananas, oil, egg, milk, and vanilla and mix well.

3 Add the wet ingredients to the dry ones and using a hand-held mixer, beat about 2 minutes until just combined.

4 Pour the batter into the prepared baking pan and bake for 24 to 26 minutes until a toothpick inserted in the middle comes out clean. Cool completely before slicing and serving.

NUTRITION PER SERVING

Calories 190
Calories from fat 44
Total fat 5g
    Saturated fat 1g
Cholesterol 28mg
Sodium 460mg
Carbohydrate 32g
    Dietary fiber 3g
    Sugars 9g
Protein 6g

Awesome Tip

When checking the labels of snack foods, look at the overall carbohydrate grams. While noting the sugar grams is important, it's the overall amount of carbohydrate that will affect your child's blood sugar. Also, look for 3 grams or more of fiber in a snack food.

CHEERY CHERRY TOMATOES

Although large tomatoes are mostly a summertime treat, good cherry tomatoes – like the ones in the mini-bucket shown here – are available all year long. Here's an easy and quick treat made with items you probably have on hand, using bite-size cherry tomatoes in a zesty marinade. The longer they marinate, the better they taste.

Serves: 6 **Serving size:** 2 or 3 tomatoes
Preparation time: 35 minutes

1 In a medium-size mixing bowl, whisk together the marinade ingredients. Add the tomatoes and allow to marinate at least 30 minutes in the refrigerator.

2 Spear the tomatoes with toothpicks, place on a platter, and serve.

Ingredients

For the marinade:

2 teaspoons olive oil

1 tablespoon balsamic vinegar

2 teaspoons dry Italian dressing mix

1 teaspoon kosher or sea salt

Freshly ground black pepper to taste

1 pint cherry tomatoes

NUTRITION
PER SERVING

Calories 34
Calories from fat 13
Total fat 1.5g
    Saturated fat 0g
Cholesterol 0
Sodium 517mg
Carbohydrate 3g
    Dietary fiber 1g
    Sugars 2g
Protein 0

FUN FRUIT PIZZAS

Fruit, you ask? Well, instead of tomato sauce and cheese, these fruity pita-bread pizzas can be put together as a dessert snack in a jiffy, without any cooking!

Serves: 2

Serving size: 1 pita

Preparation time: 2 minutes

Ingredients

¼ cup sugar-free reduced-fat vanilla yogurt

¼ teaspoon cinnamon

2 small whole-wheat pita breads, left whole

2 tablespoons diced dried fruit (such as raisins, apples, apricots, and peaches)

1 Combine the yogurt and cinnamon in a small bowl. Spread half the mixture on each pita and decorate with the dried fruit. Serve immediately.

NUTRITION PER SERVING

Calories 115
Calories from fat 7
Total fat 1g
    Saturated fat 0
Cholesterol 0

Sodium 191mg
Carbohydrate 25g
    Dietary fiber 3g
    Sugars 7g
Protein 4g

ZESTY APPLE-CHEDDAR SPREAD

Apples and cheddar cheese are two favorites among kids. They'll love the sweet taste and crunch of the apples combined with the creamy richness of the sharp cheddar cheese.

Serves: 12   **Serving size:** ½ cup
Preparation time: 30 minutes

Ingredients

1 cup reduced-fat cream cheese, softened

1 cup nonfat cottage cheese

2 medium-size apples, cored and cut into small dice

¾ cup shredded or crumbled reduced-fat sharp cheddar cheese

2 tablespoons finely chopped dates

1 Place the cream cheese and cottage cheese in a blender or food processor and pulse several times until smooth. Transfer to a medium-size mixing bowl and stir in the remaining ingredients. Cover and chill for about 2 hours (longer if necessary).

2 Serve the spread with whole-grain crackers, or with raw vegetables and apple wedges as a dip.

NUTRITION
PER SERVING

Calories 96
Calories from fat 46
Total fat 5g
    Saturated fat 3g
Cholesterol 17mg
Sodium 189mg
Carbohydrate 7g
    Dietary fiber 1g
    Sugars 4g
Protein 6g

TOTALLY TROPICAL HAWAIIAN PIZZA

Although it's always considered an odd combination for pizza, there's no denying that the combination of ham and pineapple really works.

Ingredients

2 whole-wheat English muffins, split

⅓ cup marinara sauce

4 oz. lean ham

4 pineapple rings

¼ cup shredded reduced-fat mozzarella cheese

Serves: 4

Serving size: ½ muffin

Preparation time: 5 minutes

Cooking time: 8 minutes

NUTRITION PER SERVING

Calories 159	Sodium 545mg
Calories from fat 28	Carbohydrate 23g
Total fat 3g	Dietary fiber 2g
Saturated fat 1g	Sugars 9g
Cholesterol 17mg	Protein 10g

1 Preheat the oven to 375°.

2 Place the split muffins cut side up on a baking sheet. Spread the marinara evenly over each and top with the ham, pineapple, and a sprinkling of cheese.

3 Bake the pizzas about 8 minutes until they're well heated throughout and the cheese has melted. Serve immediately.

TEMPTING TUNA DIP

Serves: 6

Serving size: 2 to 3 tablespoons

Preparation time: 20 minutes

Ingredients

1 can (6 oz.) solid white tuna in water, drained and flaked

2 tablespoons low-fat mayonnaise

2 tablespoons plain low-fat yogurt

½ cup finely shredded reduced-fat cheddar cheese

½ medium-size apple, peeled, cored, and coarsely grated

NUTRITION PER SERVING

Calories 88	Sodium 226mg
Calories from fat 41	Carbohydrate 3g
Total fat 5g	Dietary fiber 0
Saturated fat 2g	Sugars 2g
Cholesterol 20mg	Protein 9g

If you've ever been greeted with a shrill "Sandwiches again?" here's a happy and healthy alternative. Try this fruity and tangy mix of tuna and other yummy ingredients for a fast afternoon treat.

1 In a medium-size mixing bowl, combine all the ingredients, stir well, cover, and refrigerate until ready to serve. Provide raw vegetables or whole-grain crackers for dipping or spreading.

Awesome Tip: Always have snacks waiting in the refrigerator ready to go. Cut-up raw vegetables, small packages of grapes, individual yogurt cups, and cottage cheese make great snacks. Life becomes so much easier when healthy snacks are ready and available.

MORE-THAN-S'MORES PEANUTTY WAFERS

Serves: 8

Serving size: 1 wafer sandwich

Preparation time: 10 minutes

Ingredients

½ cup reduced-fat peanut butter

¼ cup reduced-carb chocolate syrup

2 tablespoons chopped peanuts

16 graham cracker squares

NUTRITION PER SERVING

Calories 226	Sodium 267mg
Calories from fat 84	Carbohydrate 30g
Total fat 9g	Dietary fiber 2g
Saturated fat 2g	Sugars 13g
Cholesterol 0	Protein 7g

Chocolate and peanut butter are a winning combination. Try this version for a s'mores-like treat without all the sugar.

1 In a small mixing bowl, combine the peanut butter, chocolate syrup, and peanuts. Spread evenly over 8 of the crackers and top with the remaining crackers. Serve immediately.

Awesome Tip
Soy nut butter, available at many supermarkets, may be used in place of peanut butter for those with peanut allergies.

OUT-OF-THIS-WORLD STRAWBERRY-AND-HAM BITES

What goes better with ham than mustard and strawberries? No kidding – just give it a try.

Serves: 6

Serving size: 2 strawberries

Preparation time: 10 minutes

Ingredients

12 large strawberries, washed and dried, with leaves left attached

1 tablespoon honey mustard

12 low-fat ham slices, cut paper-thin

1 Spread each strawberry with ¼ teaspoon of the mustard. Wrap a slice of ham around each strawberry and secure with a toothpick. Remove the toothpick before serving.

NUTRITION
PER SERVING

Calories 61
Calories from fat 16
Total fat 2g
    Saturated fat .5g
Cholesterol 20mg
Sodium 543mg
Carbohydrate 5g
    Dietary fiber 1g
    Sugars 3g
Protein 7g

Awesome Tip: Plan snacks as you would plan meals. If kids find snacks waiting when they return home, they're more likely to eat better. Organize snacks so there's something different each day.

HAMMING-IT-UP ALMOND MOUSSE

This is another simple recipe that combines creamy and crunchy textures. Try this with your favorite dipping veggie for a light, fluffy, and flavorful snack. If you can find it, fig jam adds a wonderful flavor.

1 In a food processor or blender, combine all the ingredients and process about 1 minute until smooth. Serve with carrot or celery sticks or whole-grain crackers.

Serves: 6

Serving size: 2 to 3 tablespoons

Preparation time: 15 minutes

Ingredients

2 tablespoons sliced almonds, toasted

¼ pound low-fat ham, diced

3 oz. reduced-fat cream cheese, softened

1 tablespoon lemon juice

1 tablespoon fig jam (optional)

NUTRITION PER SERVING

Calories 89	Sodium 55mg
Calories from fat 45	Carbohydrate 5g
Total fat 5g	Dietary fiber 1g
Saturated fat 2g	Sugars 3g
Cholesterol 26mg	Protein 8g

"THAT REALLY IS ITALIAN" INCREDIBLE ITALIAN DIP

Not all kids crave sweets. Some prefer a savory snack when hunger hits. After a long day at school, children will love this cheesy and savory dip spread on a vegetable or breadstick.

Serves: 6

Serving size: 2 to 3 tablespoons

Preparation time: 20 minutes

Ingredients

½ cup part-skim ricotta cheese

¼ cup low-fat cottage cheese

2 tablespoons low-fat mayonnaise

2 tablespoons plain nonfat yogurt

8 sun-dried tomatoes, softened and chopped

½ teaspoon dried basil

Salt and pepper to taste

1 In a food processor or blender, combine all the ingredients and process until smooth. Serve with raw vegetables or whole-grain breadsticks.

NUTRITION PER SERVING

Calories 56	Sodium 186mg
Calories from fat 30	Carbohydrate 4g
Total fat 3g	Dietary fiber 1g
Saturated fat 1g	Sugars 3g
Cholesterol 11mg	Protein 4g

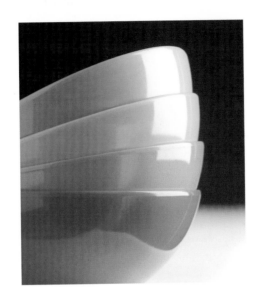

The Main Event

WHAT'S FOR DINNER?"

Solve the "What's for dinner?" dilemma once and for all. The toughest part of satisfying a child's appetite seems to occur during the dinner hour itself. Even with the least finicky eater, it can be a challenge to come up with meals that fit your diabetic child's special needs while also satisfying the rest of the family. It's not necessary to run a restaurant and exhaust yourself in your quest to make everyone happy. With the meals in this chapter, the same food will work beautifully for everyone.

There's enough variety here to cover all interests. From chicken dishes to vegetarian, you're sure to find something appetizing. But as a backup plan, do have other simple foods that can be prepared in a jiffy if your child refuses what's been prepared. A simple low-fat grilled cheese sandwich, a bowl of chicken noodle soup, or a low-fat peanut-butter sandwich can be used as a last-minute substitute.

But why not make dinnertime a real family affair? Have your kids participate in the entire process (assigning age-appropriate tasks to each). Have them help plan the family meal, draw up the grocery list, go to the store, unpack the groceries, and then prepare the meal with you (or by themselves, if they're old enough). When children are more aware of the effort that goes into preparing food, they're more likely to appreciate the meal.

Don't underestimate your child's taste. For example, this chapter includes a number of fish recipes. If you don't serve fish to your family because you believe your child won't eat it, you'll miss an opportunity to broaden your child's sense of culinary adventure. It's usually not the food itself that causes the dislike but the way it may be prepared. These recipes consider a child's palate first and foremost. And even if a new recipe meets with resistance on the first try, give it time and then try it again. It's the only way to open children's minds to a greater variety of foods. Before you know it, they'll be eagerly digging in before the plate hits the table!

TEX-MEX PIZZA

How do I make pizza? Let me count the ways. There's no time for a siesta with this quick and easy pizza. It's great for a sports-practice night and can be assembled ahead and popped into the oven when you get home.

Serves: 8

Serving size: 1 slice

Preparation time: 15 minutes

Cooking time: 20 minutes

Ingredients

1 lb. lean ground turkey

1 teaspoon cumin

1 teaspoon chili powder

Salt and pepper to taste

1 large prebaked pizza crust, such as Boboli

1½ cups mild salsa

⅔ cup shredded, reduced-fat Monterey Jack cheese

2 medium-size plum tomatoes, seeded and coarsely chopped

1 Preheat the oven to 450°.

2 In a large skillet or frying pan, cook the ground beef over medium-high heat for about 6 minutes until it's no longer pink, stirring often and breaking up any lumps. Pour off any drippings and stir in the cumin, chili powder, salt, and pepper. Set aside.

3 Place the pizza crust on a large cookie sheet and spread the salsa evenly over the crust. Sprinkle half the cheese on top of the salsa, then distribute the cooked beef over that. Sprinkle the remaining cheese over the beef, and top with the tomatoes.

4 Bake for about 12 minutes, until the crust is crispy and the cheese has melted. Let rest for 2 minutes, then slice and serve.

NUTRITION PER SERVING

Calories 303	Sodium 740mg
Calories from fat 95	Carbohydrate 26g
Total fat 8g	Dietary fiber 1g
Saturated fat 3g	Sugars 1g
Cholesterol 49mg	Protein 24g

WORRY-FREE WEEKEND PIZZA SQUARES

When you have a little more time on the weekend and want to plan a family activity in the kitchen, these pizzas will have everyone getting into the act. They can be made with white or whole-wheat pizza dough. Quick and easy, they'll quickly put that frozen pizza in a box to shame.

Serves: 8

Serving size: 1 slice

Preparation time: 20 minutes

Cooking time: 15-20 minutes

Ingredients

- 1 package (10 oz.) of refrigerated pizza dough, such as Pillsbury

- 6 slices (2 oz. each) lean, low-salt ham

- 6 tablespoons commercial marinara sauce

- ½ cup shredded part-skim mozzarella

- 1 small zucchini, trimmed and diced

1 Preheat the oven to 400°.

2 On a lightly floured surface, unroll the pizza dough and flatten into a rectangle (about 10 x 12 inches). Using a sharp knife or pizza cutter, divide the dough into 6 even portions.

3 Lay a piece of ham over each piece of dough and spread a tablespoon of marinara sauce on top. Evenly sprinkle the cheese and zucchini over all, and transfer, with a spatula, to a large cookie sheet.

4 Bake the pizzas until the crusts are golden brown and the cheese has melted, 15 to 20 minutes. Let rest 2 minutes before serving.

NUTRITION PER SERVING

Calories 226
Calories from fat 76
Total fat 8.5g
    Saturated fat 2.5g
Cholesterol 36mg
Sodium 748
Carbohydrate 23g
    Dietary fiber 1g
    Sugars 2g
Protein 16g

PIZZAZZY PASTA PIZZA

Here's another version of everyone's favorite dish – except this time we'll "hold the dough." Instead, a noodle-shaped pasta becomes the pizza crust. Try ziti, corkscrew, or even egg noodles.

Serves: 8

Serving size: 1 wedge

Preparation time: 20 minutes

Cooking time: 30 minutes

Ingredients

Cooking spray

2 cups cooked pasta or noodles

2 eggs, slightly beaten

½ cup fat-free milk

1 cup shredded part-skim mozzarella cheese, divided

1 teaspoon dry Italian seasoning

1½ cups marinara sauce

2 oz. sliced turkey or veggie pepperoni

1 Preheat the oven to 350°. Coat a 12-inch pizza pan with cooking spray.

2 In a medium-size bowl, combine the cooked pasta, eggs, milk, ½ cup of the cheese, and the Italian seasoning. Spread the mixture evenly in the pizza pan and bake for 20 minutes.

3 Remove the pan from the oven and spread the marinara sauce evenly over the pasta crust. Top with the remaining cheese and pepperoni, and continue to bake for about 10 minutes, until the cheese is melted and the pizza is heated throughout. Cut into 8 wedges and serve immediately.

NUTRITION PER SERVING

Calories 300	Sodium 496mg
Calories from fat 48	Carbohydrate 47g
Total fat 5g	Dietary fiber 2.5g
Saturated fat 3g	Sugars 5g
Cholesterol 71mg	Protein 16g

BUCKING BRONCO BBQ BEEF SANDWICHES

It will be easy to round up hungry little buckaroos with this hearty western classic. It's simple yet saucy, and that's no bull!

Serves: 4

Serving size: 1 sandwich

Preparation time: 15 minutes

Cooking time: 18 minutes

Ingredients

Barbecue Sauce:

½ cup low-sodium ketchup

1 tablespoon red wine vinegar

2 teaspoons brown sugar

½ teaspoon ground ginger

½ teaspoon Dijon mustard

---

2 boneless sirloin steaks (8 oz. each), trimmed of fat

4 whole-wheat sandwich buns

1 Preheat an oven broiler or outdoor grill.

2 In a small saucepan, stir together the barbecue sauce ingredients over medium heat and bring to a boil. Reduce the heat to low and simmer for 10 minutes. Remove from the heat and set aside.

3 Place the steak on a foil-lined broiler pan or directly on a well-oiled grill rack. Broil or grill until the steaks are cooked to medium-well, 4 to 5 minutes per side, occasionally basting with the barbecue sauce. Remove the steaks from the heat source and let rest for 5 minutes.

4 Thinly slice the meat and divide evenly among the sandwich buns. Serve immediately.

NUTRITION PER SERVING

Calories 355	Sodium 418mg
Calories from fat 79	Carbohydrate 32g
Total fat 9g	Dietary fiber 3g
Saturated fat 3g	Sugars 13g
Cholesterol 62mg	Protein 38g

HERE'S-THE-BEEF – AND FRUIT – KEBABS

Sweet and succulent, these are great year-round kebabs. On the grill or under the broiler, they offer a taste of the Mediterranean any time of year.

Serves: 8

Serving size: 1 kebab

Preparation time: 20 minutes

Cooking time: 6 to 8 minutes

Ingredients

2 tablespoons lime juice

2 garlic cloves, peeled and minced

Salt and pepper to taste

1 lb. lean sirloin steak, trimmed of fat and cut into 1-inch cubes

12 dried apricots

1 cup boiling water

1 Preheat an oven broiler or outdoor grill.

2 In a small mixing bowl, stir together the lime juice, garlic, salt, and pepper. Add the beef cubes and toss to coat. Set aside to marinate.

3 Meanwhile, put the apricots in a small bowl and pour the boiling water over them. Set them aside to soften for 10 minutes, then drain.

4 Alternately thread the beef and apricots onto 6 metal skewers (or bamboo skewers that have been soaked in water for 30 minutes). Place the kebabs on a foil-lined broiler tray or directly on a well-oiled grill rack and cook 3 to 4 minutes per side or to desired doneness. Let rest 2 minutes, then serve.

NUTRITION PER SERVING

Calories 270	Sodium 114mg
Calories from fat 87	Carbohydrate 11g
Total fat 9g	Dietary fiber 1g
Saturated fat 3g	Sugars 0
Cholesterol 62mg	Protein 26g

BOLD, BRASSY, AND BEEFY SKILLET PASTA

You can beef up pasta of almost any shape in this super skillet supper. It's a hearty, beefy flash in the pan.

Serves: 6

Serving size: ½ cup

Preparation time: 15 minutes

Cooking time: 20 minutes

Ingredients

2 teaspoons olive oil

½ small onion, peeled and minced

3 garlic cloves, peeled and minced

2½ cups chopped tomatoes, drained

1 tablespoon tomato paste

Salt and pepper to taste

1 lb. lean ground beef

8 oz. dry corkscrew pasta, cooked according to package directions

¼ cup Parmesan cheese

NUTRITION PER SERVING

Calories 281	Sodium 325mg
Calories from fat 52	Carbohydrate 35g
Total fat 6g	Dietary fiber 3g
Saturated fat 2g	Sugars 6g
Cholesterol 43mg	Protein 24g

1 Heat the oil in a large skillet over medium-high heat. Add the onion and garlic and cook for about 5 minutes, stirring occasionally, until softened. Add the beef and cook for about 5 minutes, breaking up any lumps, until the meat is no longer pink.

2 Stir in the tomatoes, tomato paste, salt, and pepper. Reduce the heat to low and simmer, stirring occasionally, for 10 minutes.

3 Add the cooked pasta and stir well to coat. Continue cooking about 2 minutes, until piping hot.

4 Top each serving with a sprinkle of Parmesan cheese.

EXTREMELY EASY ITALIAN STEAK

If you've ever been disappointed in the veal Parmesan you ordered at a restaurant, here's a succulent and satisfying variation you can make at home. This tender steak with a light crisp coating can also be served on a whole-wheat bun for an authentic and healthy steak sandwich. Now that's Italian!

Serves: 8

Serving size: 1 steak

Preparation time: 15 minutes

Cooking time: 5 to 6 minutes

Ingredients

4 beef cube steaks

Salt and pepper to taste

½ cup egg substitute

2 tablespoons water

1 cup Italian flavored breadcrumbs

2 tablespoons Parmesan cheese

2 teaspoons olive oil

1 medium-size tomato, seeded and chopped to garnish

1 In a shallow bowl, beat together the egg substitute and water. In another shallow bowl, combine the crumbs and cheese. Season each steak with salt and pepper.

2 Dip each steak first in the egg mixture, then in the breadcrumb-cheese mixture, coating well, and place on a sheet of waxed paper.

3 Heat the oil in a large nonstick skillet over medium-high heat. Add the steaks in 2 batches and cook each for 5 to 6 minutes, turning once. Add a bit more oil if necessary to prevent sticking. Transfer to a paper towel to drain.

4 Garnish each steak with chopped tomato before serving.

NUTRITION PER SERVING

Calories 345	Sodium 702mg
Calories from fat 102	Carbohydrate 16g
Total fat 12g	Dietary fiber 1g
Saturated fat 4g	Sugars 3g
Cholesterol 29mg	Protein 20g

ROTINI WITH VEGETABLE-TOMATO SAUCE

Serves: 4

Serving size: 1 cup

Preparation time: 20 minutes

Cooking time: 50 minutes

Ingredients

2 teaspoons olive oil

1 medium-size onion, peeled and diced

2 garlic cloves, peeled and minced

1 can (14 oz.) crushed tomatoes

3 tablespoons tomato paste

½ tablespoon sugar

Salt and pepper to taste

1 small zucchini, trimmed and diced

1 medium-size carrot, peeled and diced

8 oz. rotini pasta, cooked according to package directions and drained

¼ cup grated Parmesan cheese

When the cupboard seems bare, you need only a few ingredients to pull this saucy dish together. Serve with a tossed salad, and you have a quick and healthy weekday meal.

1 Heat the oil in a large nonstick skillet over medium-high. Add the onion and garlic and cook them about 5 minutes until softened, stirring occasionally. Stir in the tomatoes, tomato paste, sugar, salt, and pepper and bring to a boil. Reduce the heat to low and simmer for 20 minutes.

2 Add the zucchini and carrots and continue to simmer about 15 minutes until the vegetables are tender.

3 Add the cooked pasta to the sauce and stir well to coat. Continue to heat a few minutes more, if necessary, and serve immediately, topped with a sprinkling of Parmesan cheese.

NUTRITION PER SERVING	Total fat 5g	Carbohydrate 58g
	Saturated fat 1.5g	Dietary fiber 7g
Calories 330	Cholesterol 4mg	Sugars 8g
Calories from fat 44	Sodium 275mg	Protein 13g

ZANY ZITI BAKE

For a quick but filling dinner, try this pasta dish made with both sausage and ground beef. You can always use mild turkey sausage, but if your child prefers it spicy, go for it with hot turkey sausage.

Serves: 8

Serving size: 1 cup

Preparation time: 30 minutes

Cooking time: 50 minutes

Ingredients

½ lb. Italian turkey sausage, casings removed

¼ lb. lean (98%) ground beef

2 cups marinara sauce

1½ cups shredded part-skim mozzarella cheese

8 oz. ziti pasta, cooked according to package directions and drained

2 tablespoons grated Parmesan cheese

NUTRITION PER SERVING

Calories 246	Sodium 663mg
Calories from fat 70	Carbohydrate 27g
Total fat 7g	Dietary fiber 2g
Saturated fat 2g	Sugars 4g
Cholesterol 39mg	Protein 18g

1 Preheat the oven to 350°.

2 In a large nonstick skillet or frying pan, cook the sausage and beef over medium-high heat for about 7 minutes, stirring often and breaking up any lumps, until the meat is no longer pink. Transfer the mixture to a large mixing bowl.

3 Add the marinara sauce, 1 cup of the mozzarella, and the cooked pasta to the meat mixture and stir to combine. Spoon into a 3-quart baking dish, cover with foil, and bake for 30 minutes.

Awesome Tip: Prepare double the amount of dinner foods so that you also can pack them into your child's lunches. You'll save loads of time.

LAZY LIGHT LASAGNA ROLL-UPS

Take a break from the usual heavy, layered lasagna with these lighter roll-ups that will earn any Italian grandmother's approval. This recipe is a winner, with a rich, cheesy filling that satisfies all members of the family.

Serves: 6

Serving size: 1 roll

Preparation time: 30 minutes

Cooking time: 35 minutes

Ingredients

For the filling:

1 cup part-skim ricotta cheese

¼ lb. firm tofu, mashed

3 tablespoons grated Parmesan cheese

1 teaspoon each dried oregano, basil, and thyme

Salt and pepper to taste

---

2 cups marinara sauce

6 lasagna noodles, cooked according to package directions, drained, and rinsed under cold water

½ cup shredded part-skim mozzarella cheese

1 Preheat the oven to 400°.

2 In a medium-size mixing bowl combine all the filling ingredients. Spread 1 cup of the sauce in the bottom of a square, 8-inch baking dish.

3 Place the lasagna noodles on a clean surface or cutting board, and spread some of the filling on top of each. Roll up the lasagna jelly-roll style and place each roll seam side down in the baking dish. Spoon the remaining sauce over and top with the mozzarella cheese.

4 Cover with foil and bake for 20 minutes. Remove the foil and continue to bake about 15 minutes until the sauce is bubbly and the cheese has melted.
Serve immediately.

Awesome Tip
Some of the new low-carbohydrate pastas are quite good.
Give one a try for this dish.

NUTRITION PER SERVING

Calories 250
Calories from fat 74
Total fat 8g
    Saturated fat 4g
Cholesterol 24mg
Sodium 521mg
Carbohydrate 31g
    Dietary fiber 3g
    Sugars 4g
Protein 14g

OVER-THE-RAINBOW CREAMY BOWTIES

Ingredients

For the vegetable mixture:

2 teaspoons olive oil

1 small red bell pepper, trimmed, cored, and sliced into thin strips

1 medium-size carrot, peeled and thinly sliced

1 cup small broccoli florets

For the cream sauce:

2 teaspoons canola oil

1 tablespoon all-purpose flour

2 cups 1% milk

¼ teaspoon ground nutmeg

Salt and pepper to taste

¾ cup shredded reduced-fat cheddar cheese

2 tablespoons grated Parmesan cheese

8 oz. bowtie pasta, cooked according to package directions and drained

Bowties are optional, but the multicolored veggies are a feast for the eye and tastebuds. There's nothing formal about this simple yet healthful dish, so any fun-shaped pasta can be used.

Serves: 6

Serving size: 1 cup

Preparation time: 20 minutes

Cooking time: 20 minutes

1 Prepare the vegetable mixture: Heat the olive oil in a large skillet over medium-high heat. Add the pepper and carrot and cook about 5 minutes, stirring occasionally, until softened. Stir in the broccoli, cover with a lid, reduce the heat to low, and allow to cook until the florets are tender-crisp. Remove from the heat and set aside.

2 Prepare the cream sauce: Heat the canola oil in a medium-size saucepan over medium heat. Stir in the flour and cook about 3 minutes, stirring constantly, until the mixture begins to bubble but not brown. Gradually whisk in the milk and continue whisking constantly until the sauce is smooth and somewhat thickened (able to coat the back of a spoon). Add the nutmeg, salt, and pepper to taste and remove from the heat. Immediately add the cheeses and whisk until smooth.

3 Add the vegetable mixture and cooked pasta to the sauce and stir well to combine. Reheat on low, if necessary, and serve immediately.

NUTRITION PER SERVING

Calories 261
Calories from fat 72
Total fat 8g
    Saturated fat 3g
Cholesterol 15mg
Sodium 213mg
Carbohydrate 36g
    Dietary fiber 2g
    Sugars
Protein 13

BIG EASY MARDI GRAS PARTY RICE

Serves: 6

Serving size: 1 cup

Preparation time: 30 minutes

Cooking time: 30 minutes

Ingredients

1 lb. lean ground beef

½ large onion, peeled and diced

1 medium-size celery stalk, trimmed and diced

1 garlic clove, peeled and minced

1 medium-size green bell pepper, trimmed, cored, and diced

1 cup low-fat, reduced-sodium beef broth

2 teaspoons Worcestershire sauce

1 teaspoon each dried thyme and basil

Salt and pepper to taste

Tabasco sauce to taste

2 scallions, trimmed and minced

1 cup long-grain white or brown rice, cooked according to package directions

Try this party-in-a-dish using either brown or white rice. Or add your own flair and make a vegetarian version by substituting a can of black beans for the ground beef.

1 In a large skillet over medium-high heat, cook the beef, onion, celery, and garlic for about 7 minutes, stirring often and breaking up any lumps, until the vegetables have softened and the beef is no longer pink.

2 Stir in all remaining ingredients except the rice, bring to a simmer, cover, and cook on low, stirring occasionally, for 20 minutes.

3 Add the vegetable mixture and cooked rice to the sauce and stir well to combine. Reheat on low, if necessary, and serve immediately.

NUTRITION
PER SERVING

Calories 280
Calories from fat 61
Total fat 7g
    Saturated fat 3g
Cholesterol 67mg
Sodium 151mg
Carbohydrate 28g
    Dietary fiber 3g
    Sugars 2g
Protein 26g

EVERY-NIGHT PORK LO MEIN

Serves: 4

Serving size: 1 cup

Preparation time: 30 minutes

Cooking time: 10 minutes

Ingredients

For the sauce:

¾ cup low-fat, reduced-sodium chicken broth

1 tablespoon reduced-sodium soy sauce

1 teaspoon peeled and grated fresh gingerroot

½ teaspoon sesame oil

2 teaspoons cornstarch

---

1 teaspoon canola oil

12 oz. pork tenderloin, trimmed of fat and cut into ¼-inch strips

2 medium-size carrots, peeled and thinly sliced

1 medium red bell pepper, trimmed, cored, and thinly sliced

2 garlic cloves, peeled and minced

4 oz. cooked wide lo mein or udon noodles

Always keep a supply of packaged, cooked Asian noodles on hand, and you'll be able to whip up this dish whenever you have the urge for takeout. This tasty and easy stir-fry provides the flavor of your favorite Asian restaurant with the healthiest ingredients. Practice using your chopsticks! (But a fork works, too.)

1 Prepare the sauce: In a small mixing bowl, whisk together all the ingredients and set aside.

2 Heat the oil in a wok or large, heavy skillet over medium-high heat. Add the pork and stir-fry about 4 minutes until lightly browned and no longer pink. Remove the pork with a slotted spoon and set aside.

3 Add the carrot, red pepper, and garlic to the hot pan and stir-fry until tender-crisp, about 4 minutes. Stir in the sauce and cook until slightly thickened, 1 to 2 minutes. Add the cooked noodles and pork, toss well to coat, and continue cooking about 2 minutes more until heated through. Serve immediately.

Awesome Tip
If Asian noodles are not available, try whole-wheat spaghetti or fettucine for added fiber.

NUTRITION PER SERVING

Calories 289	Sodium 234mg
Calories from fat 61	Carbohydrate 28g
Total fat 7g	Dietary fiber 5g
Saturated fat 2g	Sugars 4g
Cholesterol 72mg	Protein 30g

TOMATOEY PORK-AND-PASTA PLATE

Serves: 4

Serving size: 1 cup

Preparation time: 30 minutes

Cooking time: 30 minutes

Ingredients

¾ lb. boneless pork tenderloin, trimmed of fat and cut into ½-inch thick medallions

1 teaspoon dried oregano

Salt and pepper to taste

2 teaspoons olive oil

1 medium-size onion, peeled and diced

1 medium-size red bell pepper, trimmed, cored, and diced

½ small zucchini, trimmed and diced

1 can (14 oz.) diced tomatoes with Italian herbs

1 tablespoon tomato paste

8 oz. fun-shaped pasta, such as wagon wheels

2 tablespoons grated Parmesan cheese

Tomatoes and pork make for a perfect pair. Just add pasta and you can't go wrong. You can quickly toss together this lean dish full of protein and tender veggies. Use fun-shaped pasta, and the kids are sure to squeal for more.

1 Sprinkle the pork medallions with the oregano, salt, and pepper.

2 Heat the oil in a large nonstick skillet over medium-high heat and add the pork medallions in a single layer. Cook until lightly browned, 3 to 4 minutes per side. Remove the pork from the skillet and set aside.

3 Add the onion and pepper to the skillet and cook over medium heat for about 5 minutes, stirring occasionally, until softened. Add the zucchini and cook for 3 more minutes. Add the tomatoes and tomato paste and bring to a boil. Reduce the heat to low and simmer for 10 minutes.

4 Return the pork to the skillet, cover with a lid, and simmer over medium-low heat for 3 minutes

5 To serve, spoon the pork and sauce over the hot cooked pasta and sprinkle with Parmesan cheese.

NUTRITION PER SERVING

Calories 403
Calories from fat 62

Total fat 7g
    Saturated fat 2g
Cholesterol 50mg
Sodium 630mg

Carbohydrate 57g
    Dietary fiber 4g
    Sugars 12g
Protein 28g

PATSY'S PORK CHOPS WITH BACON AND ONIONS

Our old friend Patsy showed us that pork loin chops can be perfectly juicy and moist when quickly pan-seared. Topped with sweet caramelized onions and a hint of smoky bacon, it's surely eating high off the hog.

Serves: 4

Serving size: 1 pork chop

Preparation time: 15 minutes

Cooking time: 15 minutes

Ingredients

2 slices reduced-sodium bacon

1 large onion, peeled and thinly sliced

2 teaspoons balsamic vinegar

Cooking spray

4 boneless pork chops (4 oz. each), trimmed of excess fat

Salt and pepper to taste

1 In a large nonstick skillet over medium-high heat, fry the bacon until crisp, about 6 minutes. Drain on a paper towel, then roughly chop and set aside.

2 Add the onions to the skillet and cook 7 to 8 minutes over medium heat until softened, stirring occasionally. Stir in the balsamic vinegar and cook 1 minute more. Transfer the onions to a small bowl, add the chopped bacon, and set aside in a warm place.

3 Wipe the skillet clean with a paper towel, then coat with cooking spray. Sprinkle the pork chops with salt and pepper and cook them in the skillet over medium-high heat until lightly browned and no longer pink inside, 4 to 5 minutes per side.

4 Top the pork chops with the bacon-and-onion mixture and serve.

NUTRITION PER SERVING

Calories 270	Sodium 400mg
Calories from fat 105	Carbohydrate 4g
Total fat 12g	Dietary fiber .5g
Saturated fat 4g	Sugars 2g
Cholesterol 89mg	Protein 29g

Awesome Tip
Try this recipe using boneless, skinless chicken breasts or even salmon steaks.

ZESTY PORK FAJITAS

The seasoning combination of these fajitas is fabulous. You can easily substitute strips of chicken or steak for the pork. Serve this with fat-free refried beans for a complete dinner that is high in protein.

Serves: 6

Serving size: 1 fajita

Preparation time: 30 minutes

Cooking time: 15 to 20 minutes

Ingredients

2 teaspoons olive oil

12 oz. pork tenderloin, trimmed of fat and cut into ¼-inch strips

1 medium green bell pepper, trimmed, cored, and thinly sliced

1 large onion, peeled and thinly sliced

1 teaspoon chili powder

Salt and pepper to taste

½ cup canned diced tomatoes, drained

6 whole-wheat flour tortillas (6 inches each)

¼ cup mild or spicy salsa

¼ cup reduced-fat sour cream

1 Preheat the oven to 350°.

2 Heat the oil in a large, heavy skillet over medium-high heat. Add the pork and cook about 5 minutes, stirring often, until lightly browned and no longer pink. Remove the pork with a slotted spoon and set aside on a warm plate.

3 Wrap the tortillas in foil and warm them in the oven for 6 minutes.

4 Add the green pepper, onion, chili powder, salt, and pepper to the skillet and cook over medium heat for about 5 minutes, stirring often, until the vegetables are softened. Stir in the chopped tomatoes, add back the cooked pork, and continue cooking another minute.

5 To serve, spoon some of the pork mixture onto a warmed tortilla, add a dollop of salsa and sour cream, and fold up the bottom and sides to make a fajita. Repeat with the remaining tortillas.

NUTRITION
PER SERVING

Calories 231
Calories from fat 75
Total fat 8g
    Saturated fat 2g
Cholesterol 49mg
Sodium 375mg
Carbohydrate 20g
    Dietary fiber 2g
    Sugars 4g
Protein 19g

TANGY PORK CUTLETS AND CHERRIES

Pork and fruit always make a great pair, but cherries don't immediately spring to mind. The cherries here add natural sweetness to the pork and make this dish pretty enough for even a holiday table.

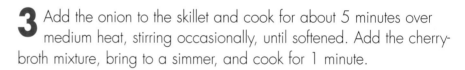

Serves: 4

Serving size: 1 pork chop

Preparation time: 15 minutes

Cooking time: 30 minutes

Ingredients

½ cup dried cherries

⅓ cup balsamic vinegar

¼ cup low-fat, reduced-sodium chicken broth

1 tablespoon brown sugar

2 teaspoons low-sodium soy sauce

1 teaspoon olive oil

4 boneless pork chops (4 oz. each) or cutlets

Salt and pepper to taste

1 small onion, peeled, halved, and thinly sliced

2 teaspoons cornstarch

1 tablespoon cold water

1 In a small bowl, combine the cherries, vinegar, broth, brown sugar, and soy sauce. Let stand for 15 minutes.

2 Meanwhile, heat the oil in a large nonstick skillet. Sprinkle the pork with salt and pepper and cook until browned over medium-high heat, 4 to 5 minutes per side. Transfer the cutlets to a clean plate and set aside.

3 Add the onion to the skillet and cook for about 5 minutes over medium heat, stirring occasionally, until softened. Add the cherry-broth mixture, bring to a simmer, and cook for 1 minute.

4 In a small custard dish, stir together the cornstarch and water until dissolved, then stir the mixture into the sauce. Cook for about 2 minutes, stirring often, until somewhat thickened. Place the cooked cutlets in the sauce, turn to coat, and cook on low until heated through, 1 minute more.

5 Serve each cutlet topped with a spoonful of the cherry sauce.

NUTRITION PER SERVING	Total fat 7g	Carbohydrate 22g
	Saturated fat 1g	Dietary fiber 2g
Calories 260	Cholesterol 70mg	Sugars 15g
Calories from fat 59	Sodium 240mg	Protein 26g

I-MADE-IT-MYSELF PORK FRIED RICE

Serves: 5

Serving size: ¾ cup

Preparation time: 30 minutes

Cooking time: 20 minutes

Ingredients

2 teaspoons peanut oil

2 scallions, trimmed and sliced

½ medium-size celery stalk, trimmed and diced

½ medium-size red bell pepper, trimmed, cored, and diced

1 garlic clove, peeled and minced

1 cup frozen peas, thawed

1 cup cubed leftover cooked pork

2 cups cooked brown or white rice, chilled for at least 4 hours

3 tablespoons reduced-sodium soy sauce

Freshly ground black pepper to taste

Cooking spray

1 large egg, beaten

This is the perfect alternative to high-sodium restaurant fried rice. You can easily substitute diced cooked chicken or small shrimp for the pork.

1 Heat the oil in a large wok or heavy skillet over medium-high heat. Add the scallions, celery, and red pepper and stir-fry about 2 minutes until tender-crisp. Add the garlic, peas, pork, and rice and stir-fry about 5 minutes until heated through. Add the soy sauce and ground pepper and cook another 2 minutes.

2 Meanwhile, in a small frying pan coated with cooking spray, scramble the egg over medium heat until cooked through. Immediately add to the fried rice, stir well, and serve.

Awesome Tip: If you have leftover rice from Chinese take-out, you can always use it at home in your own money-saving recipes for fried rice and other dishes.

NUTRITION PER SERVING

Calories 210	Sodium 395mg
Calories from fat 57	Carbohydrate 25g
Total fat 6g	Dietary fiber 3g
Saturated fat 1g	Sugars 2g
Cholesterol 67mg	Protein 14g

PORK-AND-PINEAPPLE SANDWICHES, REALLY!

Serves: 4

Serving size: 1 sandwich

Preparation time: 15 minutes

Ingredients

Sauce:

¼ cup fat-free mayonnaise

2 teaspoons Dijon mustard

1 teaspoon honey

Sandwich:

1 pound leftover roast pork loin, sliced thinly

4 oz. fat-free Swiss cheese

4 pineapple rings

4 romaine lettuce leaves

4 whole-wheat sandwich buns, split

It may sound exotic, and it is, but you'll have a taste of the islands in your hands with these sweet and succulent sandwiches. They're quick to fix for a picnic or a day in the sun.

1 In a small bowl, stir together the sauce ingredients.

2 Layer the pork, cheese, pineapple, and lettuce on the bottom halves of the buns. Spread the sauce on the top halves and close the sandwich, pressing down lightly. Cut in half, if desired, and serve immediately or wrap in plastic and refrigerate.

NUTRITION PER SERVING

Calories 444	Sodium 472
Calories from fat 90	Carbohydrate 35g
Total fat 9g	Dietary fiber 4g
Saturated fat 4g	Sugars 13g
Cholesterol 110	Protein 44g

Awesome Tip

Keep dinner balanced. Even if you don't eat much during the day, don't make the mistake of overloading on food at dinnertime. Although it's a time to be with family and relax, keep the amount of food reasonable and within the guidelines set forth by your child's dietitian.

SWEET SHRIMP ON A STICK

When grilling time is at hand, reach for the skewers. These simple and savory kebabs are created entirely with fresh ingredients. It's time to plan a luau!

Serves: 4

Serving size: 1 kebab

Preparation time: 45 minutes

Cooking time: 4 minutes

Ingredients

3 tablespoons fresh lime juice

1 tablespoon honey

1 teaspoon Dijon mustard

Salt and pepper to taste

1 pound large shrimp, peeled and deveined, tails left on

½ medium-size fresh pineapple, peeled, cored, and cut into 1-inch cubes

1 In a medium-size mixing bowl, whisk together the lime juice, honey, mustard, salt, and pepper. Add the shrimp and toss well to coat. Allow to marinate at room temperature for 15 minutes.

2 Preheat an oven broiler or outdoor grill. Thread alternating pieces of shrimp and pineapple onto 4 metal skewers (or bamboo skewers that have been soaked in warm water for 20 minutes).

3 Place the skewers on a broiler rack lined with foil or directly on a well-oiled grill rack and cook about 2 minutes per side until the shrimp is pink and the pineapple slightly browned. Serve immediately.

NUTRITION
PER SERVING

Calories 168
Calories from fat 18
Total fat 2g
    Saturated fat .5g
Cholesterol 172mg
Sodium 222mg
Carbohydrate 14g
    Dietary fiber 1g
    Sugars 10g
Protein 23g

PARMESAN BAKED CATCH OF THE DAY

Why buy frozen fish when you can serve up this simple fresh fish dish made with delicious white cod? Serve a little cocktail sauce on the side to spice it up, if you like.

Serves: 4

Serving size: 1 fillet (4 oz.)

Preparation time: 30 minutes

Cooking time: 15 minutes

Ingredients

Cooking spray

4 cod fillets (4 oz. each)

¼ cup reduced-fat mayonnaise

¼ cup grated Parmesan cheese

2 scallions, trimmed and finely sliced

2 tablespoons finely diced red bell pepper

⅓ cup Italian flavored breadcrumbs

½ teaspoon dried basil

Salt and pepper to taste

1 Preheat the oven to 400°.

2 Place the fillets in a baking dish coated with cooking spray. In a small bowl, stir together the mayonnaise, cheese, scallions, and red pepper, and spread evenly over the fillets.

3 In another small bowl, stir together the breadcrumbs, basil, salt, and pepper and sprinkle evenly over the coated fish.

4 Bake about 12 minutes until the fillets are cooked through and the crumbs are lightly browned. Serve immediately.

NUTRITION PER SERVING

Calories 177
Calories from fat 43
Total fat 5g
    Saturated fat 2g
Cholesterol 53mg
Sodium 546mg
Carbohydrate 10g
    Dietary fiber 1g
    Sugars 2g
Protein 23g

NUTTY PECAN-CRUSTED TILAPIA

Tilapia has been eaten since the days of ancient Egypt. It's delicious, so it's a great way to get everyone eating more lean fish. And who can resist that crunchy pecan crust?

Serves: 4

Serving size: 1 fillet (5 oz.)

Preparation time: 20 minutes

Cooking time: 10 to 12 minutes

Ingredients

4 tilapia fillets (5 oz. each)

2 tablespoons all-purpose flour

⅓ cup low-fat buttermilk

Dash of Tabasco sauce

½ cup plain dry breadcrumbs

3 tablespoons pecan pieces

½ teaspoon salt

¼ teaspoon garlic powder

¼ teaspoon freshly ground black pepper

2 teaspoons canola oil

Lemon wedges to garnish

1 Place the flour on a sheet of waxed paper. In a shallow dish, combine the buttermilk and Tabasco. In another shallow dish, combine the breadcrumbs, pecans, salt, garlic powder, and pepper and stir well.

2 Coat the fillets in the flour. After shaking off any excess flour, dip them in the buttermilk and coat them well with the breadcrumb mixture. Set them aside on a clean plate.

3 In a large nonstick skillet, heat the oil over medium-high heat. Fry the tilapia fillets until golden, 5 to 6 minutes per side. Place on a paper towel to drain, then serve immediately with the lemon wedges.

NUTRITION PER SERVING

Calories 260
Calories from fat 87
Total fat 8g
　　Saturated fat 1g
Cholesterol 72mg

Sodium 494mg
Carbohydrate 14g
　　Dietary fiber 1g
　　Sugars 2g
Protein 32g

UNDER-THE-SEA SALMON CAKES

A fisherman's delight, these salmon cakes are swimming in flavor but low in fat. Fresh or canned crab meat may be used, too.

Serves: 6

Serving size: 1 salmon cake

Preparation time: 20 minutes

Cooking time: 10 minutes

Ingredients

1 pound cooked fresh salmon, skin removed and flaked (or one 14 oz. can of salmon, drained and flaked)

24 saltine crackers, preferably whole wheat, finely crushed

1 large egg, beaten

3 tablespoons nonfat mayonnaise

1 tablespoon Dijon mustard

2 scallions, trimmed and finely chopped

¼ teaspoon Old Bay Seasoning®

2 teaspoons canola oil

1 In a medium-size mixing bowl, gently stir together the salmon, ⅔ of the crushed crackers, and all the remaining ingredients except the oil. Form mixture into 6 round cakes and set aside on a piece of waxed paper.

2 Place the remaining crushed crackers on a plate and coat both sides of each salmon cake, pressing gently to adhere. Transfer to a clean plate and refrigerate for 1 hour.

3 Heat the oil in a large nonstick skillet over medium-high heat. Fry the salmon cakes about 5 minutes per side until golden brown. Transfer to a paper towel to drain, then serve.

NUTRITION PER SERVING

Calories 173
Calories from fat 64
Total fat 7g
    Saturated fat 1.5g
Cholesterol 90mg
Sodium 517mg
Carbohydrate 9g
    Dietary fiber 1g
    Sugars 1g
Protein 17g

VERY TERIYAKI SHRIMP

Wok this way! The simple and savory marinade makes this stir-fry extra special. Serve over Positively Peanutty Noodles (page 48) for a real Asian meal.

1 In a medium-size mixing bowl, whisk together the soy sauce, teriyaki sauce, sesame oil, and sugar. Add the shrimp, toss well to coat, cover, and refrigerate for 1 hour, stirring occasionally.

Serves: 4

Serving size: ½ cup

Preparation time: 30 minutes

Cooking time: 5 minutes

Ingredients

3 tablespoons low-sodium soy sauce

½ cup low-sodium teriyaki sauce

1 teaspoon sesame oil

2 teaspoons brown sugar

1 pound large shrimp, peeled and deveined, tails removed

2 teaspoons peanut oil

2 scallions, trimmed and finely sliced

2 Heat the peanut oil in a wok or heavy skillet over medium-high heat. Pat the shrimp dry with a paper towel and add to the hot wok, stir-frying until the shrimp is cooked through, 3 to 5 minutes.

3 Top with the scallions and serve.

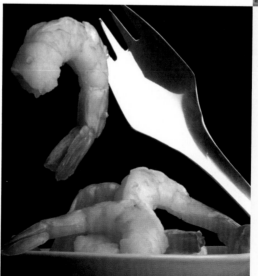

NUTRITION PER SERVING

Calories 156
Calories from fat 43
Total fat 5g
    Saturated fat 1g
Cholesterol 172mg
Sodium 685mg
Carbohydrate 6g
    Dietary fiber 0
    Sugars 4g
Protein 25g

FRESH AND FLAVORFUL FISH AND CHIPS

Ahoy, mates – come onboard with this healthful version of a famous fast food. Mild, sweet cod and crispy seasoned potatoes keep this meal anchored in flavor.

Serves: 4
Serving size: 4 oz. fish and 4 chips

Preparation time: 30 minutes
Cooking time: 40 minutes

Ingredients

For the chips:

2 teaspoons *each* paprika, garlic powder, and onion powder

Salt and pepper to taste

1 tablespoon olive oil

2 medium-size Idaho or russet potatoes, unpeeled and cut into 8 wedges each

Cooking spray

For the fish:

1 pound fresh cod, cut into 3 x 1-inch strips

¼ cup all-purpose flour

½ cup low-fat buttermilk

1 cup plain dry breadcrumbs

Salt and pepper to taste

1 tablespoon olive oil

1 Preheat the oven to 425°.

2 In a medium-size bowl whisk together the paprika, garlic and onion powders, and salt, pepper, and oil. Add the potato wedges and toss to coat. Place the potatoes in a single layer on a baking sheet coated lightly with cooking spray and bake 35 to 40 minutes, turning once, until fork-tender and crispy brown.

3 Meanwhile, place the flour in a large resealable plastic bag, pour the buttermilk into a shallow bowl, and in another shallow bowl combine the breadcrumbs, salt, and pepper. Working with a few fish strips at a time, toss them in the flour, shake off any excess, dip them in the buttermilk, and coat with the breadcrumbs. Set the strips on a clean plate and refrigerate for 20 minutes.

4 Heat the olive oil in a large nonstick skillet over medium-high heat. Fry the fish strips in a single layer until golden brown, about 3 minutes per side, then set to drain on a paper towel.

5 When the potatoes are done, serve immediately with the fish strips.

NUTRITION PER SERVING

Calories 370
Calories from fat 85
Total fat 9g
    Saturated fat 2g
Cholesterol 55mg
Sodium 286mg
Carbohydrate 43g
    Dietary fiber 4g
    Sugars 4g
Protein 27g

SOUTHWESTERN FIRECRACKER CHICKEN

If you have a hankerin' for spareribs but are also in the mood for chicken, here's the solution. One taste and you'll know this is HOT – not too spicy, but *really* good.

Serves: 6

Serving size: 1 drumstick

Preparation time: 15 minutes

Cooking time: 45 minutes

Ingredients

6 skinless chicken drumsticks

Barbecue sauce:

¼ cup firmly packed brown sugar substitute

2 teaspoons onion powder

1 teaspoon *each* celery seeds, garlic powder, and chili powder

1¼ cups low-carb ketchup

2 tablespoons white vinegar

1 tablespoon prepared mustard

1 teaspoon lemon juice

1 teaspoon liquid smoke

1 Preheat the oven to 400°.

2 Bring a large pot of water to a low simmer. Add the drumsticks and poach on very low heat for about 10 minutes. Remove the drumsticks with a pair of long-handled tongs and place them in an 8 x 8-inch baking dish.

3 Meanwhile, in a small saucepan, stir together the ingredients for the barbecue sauce. Bring to a boil, then reduce the heat to low and simmer for 10 minutes.

4 Spoon or brush half the barbecue sauce over the chicken drumsticks. Bake, turning occasionally, until the chicken is well cooked throughout, with no traces of pink.

5 Serve with the remaining barbecue sauce on the side. Use lots of napkins!

Awesome Tip

Poaching or par-cooking in water beforehand can help reduce the fat content in fatty meats such as dark-meat chicken, sausage, and beef.

NUTRITION PER SERVING

Calories 117
Calories from fat 24
Total fat 3g
    Saturated fat .5g
Cholesterol 48mg
Sodium 293mg
Carbohydrate 13g
    Dietary fiber 0
    Sugars 0
Protein 13g

"NOT-SO-SLOPPY" SLOPPY JOES

Serves: 6

Serving size: half a bun

Preparation time: 20 minutes

Cooking time: 20 minutes

Ingredients

1 pound lean ground chicken

1 small onion, peeled and finely chopped

2 garlic cloves, peeled and minced

1 teaspoon chili powder

½ teaspoon paprika

Salt and pepper to taste

1 medium-size red or green bell pepper, trimmed, cored, and finely diced

1 medium-size zucchini, trimmed and finely diced

1 can (14 oz.) diced tomatoes, drained

½ cup commercial reduced-sugar barbecue sauce

3 whole-wheat hamburger buns, split and toasted

These open-faced Joes, made with chicken, are the best things going since the original beef-based version. They're simple and delicious, not to mention healthy.
Do keep a few napkins on hand, however, just in case!

Awesome Tip: Invest in a good quality 10- or 12-inch heavy-bottom skillet. Cooking up one-pan main-course dishes can be the simplest way to get dinner on the table in a hurry.

1 In a large, heavy skillet over medium-high heat, cook the chicken with the onion, garlic, chili powder, paprika, salt, and pepper for 5 to 6 minutes until the meat is browned, stirring often and breaking up any lumps.

2 Stir in the bell pepper and zucchini and continue to cook over medium-low heat for about 5 minutes more until vegetables are tender. Add the diced tomatoes and barbecue sauce, reduce the heat to low, and simmer about 10 minutes, stirring occasionally.

3 Spoon some of the mixture over half a toasted bun and serve immediately.

NUTRITION PER SERVING

Calories 202
Calories from fat 68
Total fat 8g
    Saturated fat 2g
Cholesterol 50mg
Sodium 437mg
Carbohydrate 20g
    Dietary fiber 4g
    Sugars 6g
Protein 15g

JOHNNY APPLESEED CHICKEN-CRUNCH SALAD

When the weather is warm, why not have a cool crunchy salad for a spring or summer dinner? Just add a whole-grain roll and a low-sugar fruity dessert for a healthy light meal.

Ingredients

2 cups diced cooked chicken breast (such as Perdue Shortcuts)

1 medium-size apple, such as Yellow Delicious or Gala, cored and diced

½ medium-size celery stalk, trimmed and diced

1 scallion, trimmed and finely sliced

¼ cup raisins

⅓ cup fat-free mayonnaise

1 tablespoon low-fat sour cream

1 teaspoon lemon juice

¼ teaspoon ground cinnamon

¼ teaspoon salt

Freshly ground black pepper to taste

Lettuce leaves (optional)

Serves: 6
Serving size: ½ cup
Preparation time: 20 minutes

1 In a medium-size mixing bowl, combine the chicken, apple, celery, scallions, and raisins.

2 In a small mixing bowl, whisk together all remaining ingredients except the lettuce and pour over the chicken-apple mixture. Stir gently to coat evenly.

3 Serve immediately over the lettuce, or cover and refrigerate up to two days.

NUTRITION PER SERVING

Calories 207	Sodium 271mg
Calories from fat 60	Carbohydrate 10g
Total fat 6g	Dietary fiber 1g
Saturated fat 1g	Sugars 9g
Cholesterol 70mg	Protein 24g

HONEY-MUSTARD CRISPY-CRUST CHICKEN FINGERS

Healthier than fried, this chicken is juicy and tender with a glorious golden crust. Serve with steamed green veggies for a colorful dinner.

Serves: 4

Serving size: 3 or 4 fingers

Preparation time: 20 minutes

Cooking time: 20 minutes

Ingredients

1 tablespoon honey

1 tablespoon Dijon mustard

¼ teaspoon ground ginger

Salt and pepper to taste

1 cup cornflake crumbs

1 pound boneless, skinless chicken breasts

2 teaspoons olive oil

1 Preheat the oven to 400°.

2 In a small mixing bowl, stir together the honey, mustard, ginger, salt, and pepper. Place the cornflake crumbs in a shallow bowl.

3 Cut each chicken breast into 3 or 4 finger-size pieces. Brush each piece with the honey mixture and roll in the cornflake crumbs, coating well.

4 Place the chicken in a single layer on a nonstick baking pan and drizzle with the olive oil. Bake about 20 minutes, turning once, until the chicken is cooked through and the crust is golden brown. Serve immediately.

NUTRITION PER SERVING	
Calories 189	Sodium 251mg
Calories from fat 48	Carbohydrate 11g
Total fat 5g	Dietary fiber 0
Saturated fat 1g	Sugars 5g
Cholesterol 63mg	Protein 24g

Serves: 4

Serving size: 1 cup

Preparation time: 30 minutes

Cooking time: 12 minutes

Ingredients

For the sauce:

⅓ cup pineapple juice (from drained canned pineapple – see below)

2 tablespoons red wine vinegar

2 tablespoons sugar or Splenda

¼ teaspoon ground ginger

1 garlic clove, minced

2 teaspoons cornstarch

1 pound boneless, skinless chicken breasts, cut into 2-inch-long strips

All-purpose flour for dredging

2 teaspoons canola oil

1 small red bell pepper, trimmed, cored, and thinly sliced

1 small green bell pepper, trimmed, cored, and thinly sliced

4 scallions, trimmed and cut into 1-inch pieces

1 cup crushed pineapple or pieces, canned in their own juice and drained (juice reserved)

SOMETHING DIFFERENT SWEET-AND-SOUR PINEAPPLE CHICKEN

Although preparation time is a little longer, the brief cooking time will have this savory dish on the table in a flash. Serve with couscous instead of rice; it cooks up in just minutes and provides a different source of fiber.

1 In a small mixing bowl, whisk together the sauce ingredients and set aside.

2 Dredge the chicken strips in the flour, shaking off any excess, and set aside.

3 Heat the canola oil in a wok or large heavy skillet over medium-high heat. Add the chicken and stir-fry until no longer pink, 4 to 5 minutes. Using a slotted spoon, transfer the chicken to a clean plate.

4 Add the red and green peppers to the hot wok and stir-fry for 3 minutes. Add the scallions and stir-fry another 2 minutes.

5 Add the sauce and cook about 1 minute, stirring often, until it begins to thicken. Return the chicken to the wok, add the pineapple, and stir well to coat. Continue cooking about 1 minute more until all ingredients are heated through, and serve immediately.

NUTRITION
PER SERVING

Calories 256
Calories from fat 46
Total fat 5g
    Saturated fat 1g
Cholesterol 67mg
Sodium 64mg
Carbohydrate 25g
    Dietary fiber 2g
    Sugars 17g
Protein 26g

ZIPPY ZAPATA MEXICAN TURKEY BURGERS

When you can't decide whether you want chili, tortillas, or burgers, make it easy on yourself and have them all at once. Forming the patties into oblong shapes helps them fit easily into the tortillas for little hands to manage.

Serves: 4

Serving size: 1 burger (4 oz.)

Preparation time: 15 minutes

Cooking time: 15 minutes

Ingredients

For the burgers:

¾ pound lean ground turkey

¼ pound lean ground beef

⅓ cup mild salsa

2 tablespoons dry breadcrumbs

1 teaspoon dried oregano

¼ teaspoon dried cumin

Salt and pepper

4 flour tortillas (6 inches each)

1 cup shredded lettuce

¼ cup mild salsa

1 Preheat an oven broiler or outdoor grill. Preheat the oven to 350°.

2 In a medium-size mixing bowl, stir together the burger ingredients until very well combined. Form into four oblong patties and set aside.

3 Place the burgers on a broiler pan or directly on a well-oiled grill rack and cook for about 15 minutes, turning once, until browned and well cooked.

4 Meanwhile, wrap the tortillas in foil and heat in the oven for 8 to 10 minutes.

5 To serve, place a burger in the middle of a tortilla, top with some lettuce and salsa, and roll tightly.

NUTRITION PER SERVING

Calories 308
Calories from fat 108
Total fat 12g
  Saturated fat 3.5g

Cholesterol 92mg
Sodium 583mg
Carbohydrate 22g
  Dietary fiber 2g
  Sugars 2g
Protein 27g

Sweets and Treats

SWEETS AND TREATS

To kids (and to some adults as well), the world of sweets is something of a sacred place. Taking sweets completely away from a child with diabetes can spell only disaster. Sensitivity to sweetness is one of the first taste responses children fully develop. To attempt to deprive them of treats would be a futile task.

Fortunately, chocolate, whipped cream, and other gooey fun can still be part of life for a diabetic child. This chapter's recipes replicate the familiar flavors kids love, but their fat and carbohydrate counts are significantly lower. From puddings and cakes to cookies and bars, there's sure to be a sweet that will satisfy your child's palate. And when kids prepare dessert instead of opening a box, they learn that the quality of a homemade treat is much better for them.

Still, regard these dessert recipes as occasional treats for kids. A child should opt for a piece of fresh fruit for dessert as much as possible. Sweets need to be viewed as once-in-a while kinds of food rather than everyday fare.

Many of these desserts are prepared as individual portions, which can be a great lesson for children. Once they begin to see realistic portion sizes, weight control and other issues related to overeating become much more manageable.

So, go bake up a batch of Lipsmacking Lemon Bars or whip up some Totally Oatmeal Raisin and Peanut Butter Cookies, and watch your child's face light up with a blissful smile.

CHOCOLATE LOVER'S PEANUT-BUTTER PUDDING

Nothing goes together better than chocolate and peanut butter. If you like, you can add a small dollop of low-fat whipped topping right before serving.

Serves: 4

Serving size: ½ cup

Preparation time: 15 minutes

Ingredients

1 package (1.4 oz.) of sugar-free, fat-free instant chocolate pudding

1¾ cups fat-free milk

2 tablespoons reduced-fat peanut butter

2 tablespoons finely chopped peanuts

NUTRITION PER SERVING

Calories 118
Calories from fat 47
Total fat 5g
    Saturated fat 1g
Cholesterol 2mg
Sodium 125mg
Carbohydrate 12g
    Dietary fiber 1g
    Sugars 8g
Protein 7g

1 In a medium-size mixing bowl, using a whisk or hand-held electric mixer, beat all the ingredients together for about 2 minutes until well combined. Divide the pudding among four ½-cup dessert dishes and cover with plastic wrap. Refrigerate for 1 to 2 hours until set.

Awesome Tip: If your child requests a dessert that's particularly laden with sugar or higher in fat, you may not have to say no. Work with your child's dietitian to figure out how your child's meal plan can incorporate such requests. Perhaps a "what-I-want" dessert night is possible once a week. Talk this over with your child's health-care team and see whether together you can come up with techniques that make your child feel as normal as possible.

SUPER-APPEALING BANANA SUNDAES

Banana splits bring to mind the days of old-fashioned ice-cream shops for most adults. This version for kids is a super-healthy treat with much less sugar and fat. It's a great sundae for any day of the week.

Serves: 4

Serving size: 1 dessert dish

Preparation time: 10 minutes

Ingredients

1 cup sugar-free frozen vanilla yogurt

½ cup coarsely crushed sugar-free cookies, such as vanilla wafers or shortbread

1 medium-size banana, peeled and sliced

¼ cup frozen light whipped topping, thawed

1 Place a ¼-cup scoop of frozen vanilla yogurt in each of four 1-cup-size dessert dishes. Layer the remaining ingredients into each dish and serve immediately.

NUTRITION PER SERVING	
Calories 226	Sodium 182mg
Calories from fat 27	Carbohydrate 38g
Total fat 3g	Dietary fiber 2g
Saturated fat 1g	Sugars 9g
Cholesterol 17mg	Protein 4g

PEANUT-BUTTER AND CHOCOLATE-CHIP-COOKIE CUPCAKES

Makes: 12 muffins

Serving size: 1 muffin

Preparation time: 20 minutes

Cooking time: 17 to 20 minutes

Ingredients

Cooking spray

2 large eggs

¼ cup mashed ripe bananas

¼ cup reduced-fat peanut butter

¼ cup canola oil

1 cup fat-free milk

1 teaspoon vanilla extract

1½ cups all-purpose flour

½ cup whole-wheat flour

¼ cup Splenda for baking

1 teaspoon baking powder

¼ teaspoon baking soda

½ cup semi-sweet mini chocolate chips

¼ cup frozen light whipped topping, thawed

A chocolate-chip cookie for breakfast? That's right. That's what these cupcakes taste like, without all the fat and sugar. High in protein and healthful ingredients, they're delicious anytime.

1 Preheat the oven to 350°. Coat a 12-cup muffin pan with cooking spray.

2 In a medium-size mixing bowl, beat together the eggs, banana, peanut butter, oil, milk, and vanilla extract. In another medium-size mixing bowl, whisk together the flours, Splenda, baking powder, and baking soda. Add the wet ingredients to the dry ingredients and stir until just combined. Fold in the chocolate chips.

3 Fill each muffin cup ⅔ full with the batter. Bake 17 to 20 minutes until a toothpick inserted into the center of a cupcake comes out clean. Let rest for about 5 minutes in the pan and then transfer to a rack to cool. Store in a resealable plastic bag or airtight container and keep up to four days in the refrigerator.

NUTRITION PER SERVING		
Calories 208	Cholesterol 36mg	Carbohydrate 25g
Calories from fat 90	Sodium 130mg	Dietary fiber 2g
Total fat 10g		Sugars 6g
Saturated fat 2g		Protein 6g

JAMMIN' MINI FRUIT TARTS

As delicious as they are pretty, these little tarts will drive you crazy for fruit. Naturally sweetened, they're healthy and a cinch to make, even for a fancy event.

Makes: 15 tarts

Serving size: 1 tart

Preparation time: 20 minutes

Chill: 1 to 2 hours

Ingredients

1 package (8 oz.) reduced-fat cream cheese, softened

¼ cup no-sugar-added strawberry jam

¼ cup slivered almonds, toasted and roughly chopped

15 mini frozen phyllo-dough shells, thawed

½ cup sliced fresh strawberries

1 In a small mixing bowl, beat together the cream cheese, jam, and almonds. Divide the mixture among all the tart shells and refrigerate for 1 to 2 hours.

2 Before serving, top each tart with the sliced strawberries.

NUTRITION PER SERVING

Calories 56	Cholesterol 8mg	Carbohydrate 5g
Calories from fat 33	Sodium 57mg	Dietary fiber 0
Total fat 4g		Sugars 0
Saturated fat 2g		Protein 2g

MORE-THAN-A-TRIFLE BERRY TRIFLE

Serves: 8

Serving size: ½ cup

Preparation time: 20 minutes

Ingredients

½ loaf fat-free light pound cake

⅓ cup no-sugar-added raspberry jam

1 package (4 oz.) sugar-free, fat-free vanilla pudding, prepared according to package directions using fat-free milk

1 cup fresh blueberries, raspberries, or strawberries, or any combination

1 cup frozen light whipped topping

There's nothing trifling about this trifle. Create a colorful dessert for any occasion using a variety of fruits such as blueberries and raspberries for a Fourth of July picnic.

1 Cut the pound cake into 1-inch slices. Cut each slice in half. Spread one side of each piece with the raspberry jam.

2 In a small decorative glass bowl or trifle dish, place half the cake slices, jam side up, on the bottom and up the sides of the bowl. Spread half the pudding over the layered slices and sprinkle with half the berries. Repeat with another layer and cover the entire trifle with the whipped topping.

3 Set in the refrigerator for 1 hour, then serve.

Awesome Tip: Make dessert a yes-yes rather than a no-no. If kids see that there are appealing desserts they can eat that are healthful, chances are they won't try to sneak desserts that may be much higher in sugar, fat, and carbohydrates. Help them to see that a healthful dessert can be part of their overall food plan, even on an everyday basis.

NUTRITION PER SERVING

Calories 116
Calories from fat 8
Total fat 1g
   Saturated fat 0
Cholesterol 1mg

Sodium 121mg
Carbohydrate 26g
   Dietary fiber 1g
   Sugars 15g
Protein 3g

Calories 130
Calories from fat 57
Total fat 6g
  Saturated fat 1g
Cholesterol 0

Sodium 60mg
Carbohydrate 16g
Dietary fiber 1g
Sugars 3g
Protein 2g

"MUNCH"-ADO-ABOUT-NOTHING
APPLESAUCE MINI-MUFFINS

The "nothing" in this recipe refers to the minimum of fat. These muffins, adapted from a full-fat and full-sugar recipe, are great for after-school snacks or party treats.

Makes: 48 mini-muffins

Serving size: 2 muffins

Preparation time: 30 minutes

Cooking time: 15 to 17 minutes

Ingredients

Cooking spray

2 cups Splenda

½ cup low-fat, trans-fat-free margarine, such as Smart Balance

¼ cup canola oil

1 (4 oz.) container egg substitute

1 teaspoon vanilla extract

3 cups all-purpose flour

½ teaspoon baking soda

1¼ teaspoons ground cinnamon

¾ teaspoon ground allspice

½ teaspoon ground cloves

1 jar (24 oz.) unsweetened plain applesauce

1 Preheat the oven to 400°. Coat 2 mini-muffin tins with cooking spray.

2 In a large mixing bowl, using a hand-held electric mixer set on medium speed, beat together the margarine and Splenda for about 3 minutes until fluffy. Add the egg substitute and vanilla and beat another minute.

3 In another large mixing bowl, whisk together the flour, baking soda, and spices.

4 Add half the dry ingredients to the margarine mixture and beat until just combined, then beat in half the applesauce. Repeat with the remaining flour mixture and applesauce. Do not overbeat.

5 Fill ⅔ of each muffin cup with batter. Bake 17 to 19 minutes until lightly browned and a toothpick inserted into the center of a muffin comes out clean. Cool the muffins in the pan for 5 minutes before transferring them to a rack to cool completely. Repeat with the remaining batter.

TOTALLY OATMEAL-RAISIN-AND-PEANUT-BUTTER COOKIES

Yummy and chewy with the right amount of crunch, these cookies are packed with protein and fiber and low in fat and sugar. Have a batch of these on hand for lunchboxes or after-school treats.

Makes: about 40 cookies

Serving size: 2 cookies

Preparation time: 30 minutes

Cooking time: 7 to 9 minutes

Ingredients

½ cup unsalted butter, softened

½ cup reduced-fat peanut butter

¼ cup Splenda for baking

¼ cup firmly packed light brown sugar

½ teaspoon baking soda

2 large egg whites

1 teaspoon vanilla

1 cup all-purpose flour

1 cup quick-cooking rolled oats

½ cup raisins

1 Preheat the oven to 375°.

2 In a large mixing bowl, using a hand-held electric mixer set at medium speed, beat together the butter and peanut butter until light and fluffy. Add the Splenda, brown sugar, and baking soda and beat for 2 more minutes. Add the egg whites and vanilla and beat 1 minute more. Stir in the flour by hand until the mixture is well combined, then fold in the oats and raisins.

3 Drop the dough by rounded teaspoons 2-inches apart onto an ungreased cookie sheet. Bake 7 to 9 minutes in the middle of the oven until browned. Transfer the cookies to a wire rack to cool. Repeat with the remaining cookie dough. Store cookies in an airtight container and keep for four days at room temperature.

NUTRITION PER SERVING

Calories 145
Calories from fat 66
Total fat 7g
    Saturated fat 3.5g
Cholesterol 12mg
Sodium 89mg
Carbohydrate 17g
    Dietary fiber 1g
    Sugars 6g
Protein 3g

WHODUNNIT RASPBERRY-THUMBPRINT COOKIES

Thumbs up to these lightly sweet cookies. Use the back of a teaspoon to make the "thumbprint" if you prefer or enlist the help of little thumbs.

Makes: about 50 cookies

Serving size: 2 cookies

Preparation time: 45 minutes

Cooking time: 12 to 15 minutes

Ingredients

½ cup unsweetened applesauce

½ cup (1 stick) unsalted butter, softened

1 large egg white

1 tablespoon vanilla

½ cup Splenda for baking

3 cups all-purpose flour

1 teaspoon baking soda

¼ teaspoon salt

½ cup no-sugar-added raspberry jelly

NUTRITION PER SERVING

Calories 106	Sodium 77mg
Calories from fat 34	Carbohydrate 16g
Total fat 4g	Dietary fiber 1g
Saturated fat 2g	Sugars 3g
Cholesterol 10mg	Protein 2g

1 Preheat the oven to 350°. Coat a large cookie sheet with cooking spray.

2 In a large mixing bowl, using a hand-held electric mixer set on medium speed, beat together the applesauce and butter until fluffy. Add the egg white and vanilla and continue to beat 1 minute.

3 In a medium-size mixing bowl whisk together the Splenda, flour, baking soda, and salt, then add the flour mixture a little at a time to the butter mixture, beating well after each addition. Switch to a wooden spoon as the dough thickens.

4 Form the dough into 1-inch balls and place 2 inches apart on the prepared cookie sheet. Dip your thumb in water and make an indentation in the center of each cookie. Spoon ¼ to ½ teaspoon of the raspberry jelly onto the center of each cookie and bake 12 to 15 minutes until lightly browned. Transfer the cookies to a wire rack to cool and repeat with the remaining dough. Place in an airtight container and store at room temperature for up to four days.

I-CAN'T-BELIEVE-IT'S-A-BROWNIE PIZZA

Serves: 12

Serving size: 1 slice

Preparation time: 10 minutes

Cooking time: 20 to 25 minutes

Ingredients

1   package reduced-fat brownie mix

Cooking spray

1   tablespoon vanilla

¼ cup pecan pieces, toasted

2   cups assorted fruit such as sliced
    strawberries, kiwi, bananas,
    and peaches

½ cup sugar-free chocolate-flavored
    ice-cream topping

At your next pizza party, serve pizza for dessert, too, with this fun chocolaty version. Fruit and ice cream makes this a brownie sundae in a pizza pan.

1 Preheat the oven to 350°. Spray a 12-inch pizza pan with cooking spray.

2 Prepare the brownie mix according to package directions, adding the vanilla and pecan pieces. Spread the mixture in the prepared pan and bake 20 to 25 minutes until a toothpick inserted into the center comes out clean. Allow to cool completely in the pan.

3 Top decoratively with the sliced fruit, drizzle the chocolate topping over all, and cut with a pizza cutter to serve.

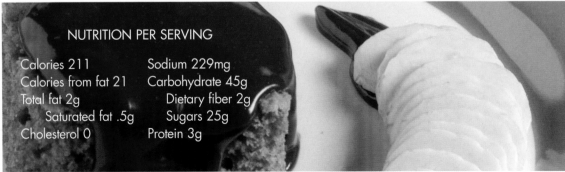

NUTRITION PER SERVING

Calories 211	Sodium 229mg
Calories from fat 21	Carbohydrate 45g
Total fat 2g	Dietary fiber 2g
Saturated fat .5g	Sugars 25g
Cholesterol 0	Protein 3g

MINI RAISIN-THE-ROOF MUFFINS

A great snack on the go, these little treats are full of sweet, juicy raisins, yet they're low in sugar and fat.

Makes: 24 mini-muffins

Serving size: 2 muffins

Preparation time: 20 minutes

Cooking time: 20 minutes

Ingredients

Cooking spray

1 cup all-purpose flour

¼ cup Splenda for baking

1 teaspoon baking powder

1 teaspoon ground cinnamon

¼ teaspoon ground cloves

¾ cup fat-free milk

¼ cup canola oil

1 large egg

1 teaspoon vanilla extract

⅓ cup raisins

1 Preheat the oven to 400°. Coat 2 mini-muffin tins with cooking spray.

2 In a medium-size mixing bowl, whisk together the flour, Splenda, baking powder, cinnamon, and cloves. In another medium-size bowl, whisk together the milk, oil, egg, and vanilla. Add the wet ingredients to the dry ingredients and stir until just combined. Fold in the raisins.

3 Fill the muffin cups about ¾ full and bake about 18 to 20 minutes until lightly browned and a toothpick inserted in the center comes out clean. Cool in the tins for 5 minutes then transfer to a rack to cool completely. Place in a resealable plastic bag or airtight container and store up to four days in the refrigerator.

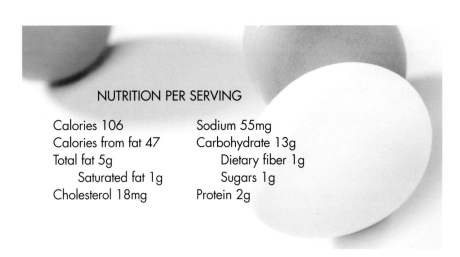

NUTRITION PER SERVING

Calories 106

Calories from fat 47

Total fat 5g

    Saturated fat 1g

Cholesterol 18mg

Sodium 55mg

Carbohydrate 13g

    Dietary fiber 1g

    Sugars 1g

Protein 2g

LIPSMACKING LEMON BARS

Makes: 18 bars

Serving size: 1 bar

Preparation time: 30 minutes

Cooking time: 20 to 25 minutes

Ingredients

Cooking Spray

For the crust:

¾ cup all-purpose flour

3 tablespoons Splenda for baking

¼ cup (½ stick) unsalted butter

For the filling:

1 large egg

1 large egg white

⅓ cup Splenda for baking

2 tablespoons all-purpose flour

2 tablespoons fresh lemon juice

1 tablespoon water

¼ teaspoon baking powder

1 teaspoon grated lemon rind

Light and lemony with a flaky crust, these luscious little bars are perfect for your next tea party. Teddy and your child's other distinguished guests will certainly approve.

1 Preheat the oven to 350°. Coat a square 8 x 8-inch baking pan with cooking spray.

2 Prepare the crust: In a small mixing bowl, combine the flour, butter, and Splenda. Using a pastry blender or the back of a fork, cut the butter into the flour until the mixture resembles coarse crumbs. Press the mixture firmly and evenly into the bottom of the prepared pan and set aside.

3 Prepare the filling: In a medium-size mixing bowl, using a hand-held electric mixer set on high speed, beat together the egg and egg white until frothy. Add the remaining ingredients and beat about 3 minutes on medium speed until well combined. Pour the filling evenly over the crust and bake for 20 to 25 minutes until the edges are brown and the filling is set.

4 Set the pan on a rack to cool completely before cutting into 18 squares. Place in an airtight container and store up to 2 days at room temperature (or freeze for up to 1 month). To defrost, place the container the refrigerator overnight.

NUTRITION
PER SERVING

Calories 53
Calories from fat 26
Total fat 3g
    Saturated fat 2g
Cholesterol 18mg
Sodium 14mg
Carbohydrate 6g
    Dietary fiber 0
    Sugars 0
Protein 1g

Rainy Weekends:
Indoor Fun

RAINY WEEKENDS: INDOOR FUN

It just isn't a day for outside play, and your child is looking for something to do. Instead of turning on the TV, think how this less-than-perfect weather has brought you a golden opportunity. Why not cook up some fun in the kitchen together? In these days of overscheduled children, why not slow down and enjoy some old-fashioned fun by preparing a healthful treat with your child? Experiences like this have an educational side as well, since kids can learn some of the basics of food preparation while creating food they most love: snacks and treats.

From sweet to savory, this chapter has it all to keep your child busy. Think of it as a chance to introduce your child to the idea of cooking. You can begin to demonstrate that even preparing dinner isn't all that intimidating. Also, if kids can realize that not all treats come ready-made from a package, they'll grow to appreciate the love and care that go into preparing food with their own two hands.

So turn this opportunity into a really enjoyable day. Have your child invite friends over to partake in the fun. Perhaps the other children will love it so much that every rainy day will become kitchen day in the neighborhood!

GOING, GOING, GONE BANANA BOATS

No one has to go overboard on fat and sugar with this boatload of tasty mini-morsels!

Serves: 2

Serving size: 1 banana

Preparation time: 5 minutes

Cooking time: 5 to 6 minutes

Ingredients

- 2 small bananas
- 1 tablespoon reduced-fat peanut butter
- 2 teaspoons peanut-butter-flavored mini-chips
- 1 tablespoon mini-marshmallows

1 Preheat the oven to 400°.

2 Peel down one strip of a banana, keeping the end of the strip attached and the rest of the peel intact. Cut a slit along the length of the exposed banana and spread the peanut butter inside. Push the chips and marshmallows into the peanut butter and fold back the peel. Repeat with the other banana.

3 Wrap each banana in foil and place on a baking sheet. Bake for 5 to 6 minutes until the bananas are hot and the chips and marshmallows have melted. Carefully unwrap the foil, pull back the peel, and serve.

NUTRITION PER SERVING

Calories 145	Sodium 75mg
Calories from fat 39	Carbohydrate 28g
Total fat 4g	Dietary fiber 4g
Saturated fat 2g	Sugars 18g
Cholesterol 0	Protein 4g

NO-BAKE FRUIT BALLS

Makes: 24 balls

Serving size: 2 balls

Preparation time: 15 minutes

Ingredients

1½ cups reduced-fat peanut butter

⅔ cup raisins

3 tablespoons honey

1½ cups shredded wheat cereal,
finely crushed

NUTRITION PER SERVING

Calories 211	Sodium 251mg
Calories from fat 21	Carbohydrate 30g
Total fat 3g	Dietary fiber 3g
Saturated fat 0g	Sugars 13g
Cholesterol 0	Protein 3g

These balls of peanutty goodness can be made well ahead and kept for whenever a case of the munchies comes along.

1 In a medium-size mixing bowl, stir together the peanut butter, raisins, and honey. Place the crushed shredded wheat in a shallow bowl.

2 Use a small melon-baller to make 24 balls of the peanut-butter mixture. Coat with the shredded wheat and set aside on a cookie sheet lined with waxed paper. Refrigerate at least 2 hours before serving.

Awesome Tip:
When the weather outside keeps your kids inside,
no couch potatoes allowed! Get your kids involved with projects,
cooking being a perfect one. And cooking does burn some calories:
on average about 75 calories an hour. It's not a lot, but it's
better than sitting in front of the TV!

"DON'T BE LEFT OUT IN THE COLD"
FROZEN-BANANA POPS

In place of frozen ice pops laden with sweeteners and artificial color, these pops are tops for a healthy snack. Kids will go bananas over them.

Serves: 8

Serving size: 1 banana pop

Preparation time: 20 minutes

Ingredients

3 tablespoons hot water

⅓ cup cocoa powder

2 teaspoons honey

8 popsicle sticks

4 bananas, peeled and cut in half crosswise

½ cup finely crushed peanuts or almonds

1 In a small mixing bowl, stir together the hot water and cocoa powder until a thick but smooth consistency is formed. Stir in the honey.

2 Insert a popsicle stick into each banana half. Roll each in the cocoa mixture and then in the nuts. Place the banana pops on a baking sheet lined with waxed paper and freeze for several hours.

3 Serve the frozen pops immediately or store each pop in a plastic baggie and keep frozen.

NUTRITION
PER SERVING

Calories 140
Calories from fat 45
Total fat 5g
    Saturated fat 1g
Cholesterol 0
Sodium 2mg
Carbohydrate 21g
    Dietary fiber 4g
    Sugars 13g
Protein 3g

CHOCOLATE FUN WITH FRUIT

Serves: 8

Serving size: ⅓ cup

Preparation time: 20 minutes

Ingredients

1 medium-size banana, peeled and cut into 1-inch chunks

1 cup cantaloupe chunks

1 cup whole strawberries

1 sugar-free chocolate bar (8 oz.)

1 tablespoon non-hydrogenated margarine

Toothpicks

A little chocolate goes a long way in this sweet yet wholesome treat. Invite the neighborhood kids over after school and let everyone take a dip.

NUTRITION PER SERVING

Calories 221
Calories from fat 141
Total fat 15g
    Saturated fat 9g
Cholesterol 0
Sodium 22mg
Carbohydrate 15g
    Dietary fiber 1g
    Sugars 5g
Protein 5g

1 Place all the fruit on a platter.

2 In the top of a double boiler, melt together the chocolate and margarine, stirring often. Remove from the heat and allow to sit for 5 minutes.

3 Meanwhile, spear each of the fruit pieces with the toothpicks. Dip the fruit in the chocolate mixture, allowing any excess to drip off. Place on a cookie sheet lined with waxed paper and refrigerate about 1 hour until set.

4 Alternatively, transfer the warm chocolate mixture to a small dipping bowl on a platter and place the speared fruit pieces decoratively around the platter. Allow the children to choose and dip their own fruit as they would into a fondue.

HIT-THE-TRAIL POPCORN-CRUNCH MIX

Serves: 8

Serving size: ⅓ cup

Preparation time: 15 minutes

Cooking time: 30 minutes

Ingredients

3 cups air-popped popcorn

2 cups whole-grain pretzel sticks

1 cup Cheerios cereal

2 tablespoons reduced-sodium
soy sauce

1 tablespoon Worcestershire sauce

2 teaspoons garlic powder

1 teaspoon onion powder

3 tablespoons non-hydrogenated
margarine, melted

Toothpicks

Trail mix and other handy snacks are a snap to make at home, and they're much more economical. Grabbing a handful of this whole-grain crunch to munch is a terrific healthy snack. Place some in a baggie and you have a healthy snack to go.

1 Preheat the oven to 300°.

2 In a large mixing bowl, combine the popcorn, pretzels, and cereal. In a small mixing bowl, whisk together the remaining ingredients and add to the large bowl, tossing well to coat. Spread the mixture out on a large baking sheet with a rim and bake about 30 minutes until lightly browned, shaking the pan occasionally. Cool completely before serving. To store, place in an airtight container or resealable plastic bag and keep at room temperature for up to one week.

NUTRITION
PER SERVING

Calories 173
Calories from fat 49
Total fat 5g
    Saturated fat 1g
Cholesterol 0
Sodium 296
Carbohydrate 29g
    Dietary fiber 3g
    Sugars 1g
Protein 4g

CRISPY CHEESE CRACKERS

Makes: 18 to 20 crackers

Serving size: 3 crackers

Preparation time: 30 minutes

Cooking time: 15 minutes

Ingredients

1 cup all-purpose flour

¼ cup toasted wheat germ

2 tablespoons grated Parmesan cheese

2 teaspoons garlic powder

2 tablespoons canola oil

⅓ cup fat-free milk

NUTRITION PER SERVING	
Calories 82	Sodium 39mg
Calories from fat 63	Carbohydrate 24g
Total fat 7g	Dietary fiber 2g
Saturated fat 1g	Sugars 2g
Cholesterol 2mg	Protein 7g

Light and crispy, these crackers packed with wholesome goodness will make you smile. Say "cheese!"

1 Preheat the oven to 325°.

2 In a medium-size mixing bowl, combine all the ingredients except the milk. Gradually stir in the milk until a soft dough forms. Turn out onto a lightly floured surface and using a floured rolling pin, roll the dough out to a ⅛-inch thickness.

3 Using a sharp knife, cut the dough into about 18 cracker squares and place on a nonstick baking sheet. Prick the crackers with a fork and bake about 15 minutes until the edges are lightly browned. Cool completely before serving. Store in an airtight container or resealable plastic bag in the refrigerator for up to one week.

MICROWAVE BEAN CHILI

Serves: 4

Serving size: ½ cup

Preparation time: 20 minutes

Cooking time: 3 minutes

Ingredients

1 cup cooked brown or white rice

½ cup canned black, pinto, or kidney beans, drained and rinsed

⅓ cup frozen corn kernels

½ cup canned diced tomatoes, drained

2 tablespoons diced red bell pepper

2 tablespoons finely minced onion

½ teaspoon chili powder

Pinch cayenne (optional)

2 tablespoons shredded reduced-fat cheddar cheese

Should chili contain beans or not? That's a question adults have been fighting over for years. Happily, however, kids will be fighting over seconds of this super crowd-pleaser.

1 In a microwave-safe container, combine all the ingredients except the cheese and stir well

2 Microwave the chili on high for 3 minutes until heated throughout. Serve immediately with a sprinkling of cheese.

NUTRITION PER SERVING

Calories 135	Sodium 93mg
Calories from fat 13	Carbohydrate 25g
Total fat 1.5g	Dietary fiber 5g
Saturated fat .5g	Sugars 5g
Cholesterol 1mg	Protein 6g

LIGHT-AS-A-FEATHER APPLE FRITTERS

You won't fritter your time away making these luscious bundles filled with crunchy apple bites. Look for fall's best variety of naturally sweet apples at your local farmers' market.

Serves: 8

Serving size: 3 fritters

Preparation time: 30 minutes

Cooking time: 6 minutes

Ingredients

4 apples, peeled, cored and cut into small dice

1 cup all-purpose flour

½ teaspoon baking powder

2 tablespoons Splenda

2 large eggs, separated

½ cup fat-free milk

Cooking spray

Sugar-free maple syrup (optional)

1 In a medium-size mixing bowl, whisk together the flour, baking powder, and Splenda. In a small mixing bowl, beat together the egg yolks and milk. Stir the egg mixture into the dry ingredients, then fold in the apples.

2 Using a hand-held electric mixer, in a medium-size mixing bowl beat the egg whites on high until they form stiff peaks. Carefully fold into the fritter mixture.

3 Coat a 12-inch nonstick skillet or griddle with cooking spray and heat over medium-high until a drop of fritter batter sizzles immediately. Drop tablespoonfuls of the batter 2 inches apart and cook until golden brown, 2 to 3 minutes per side. Transfer the fritters to a warm platter and continue with the remaining batter.

4 Serve warm with sugar-free maple syrup, if desired.

NUTRITION PER SERVING

Calories 117	Sodium 67mg
Calories from fat 13	Carbohydrate 23g
Total fat 1.5g	Dietary fiber 1g
Saturated fat .5g	Sugars 7g
Cholesterol 53mg	Protein 4g

KERPLOP CHEESE-DROP BISCUITS

Fluffy biscuits are wonderful as a snack or served with a cup of soup for lunch on a chilly day. Make a batch to store in the freezer, and then defrost and reheat them as needed.

Makes: 12 biscuits

Serving size: 1 biscuit

Preparation time: 20 minutes

Cooking time: 12 to 15 minutes

Ingredients

1 cup self-rising flour

3 tablespoons olive oil

1½ tablespoons grated
   Parmesan cheese

⅓ cup fat-free milk

1 Preheat the oven to 450°.

2 Place the flour in a small mixing bowl. Using a fork, stir in the oil until coarse crumbs form. Mix in the cheese, then add the milk a little at a time, stirring until well combined.

3 Drop the batter by heaping tablespoons onto an ungreased baking sheet and bake 12 to 15 minutes until the biscuits are lightly browned. Serve immediately.

NUTRITION
PER SERVING

Calories 73
Calories from fat 34
Total fat 4g
   Saturated fat 1g
Cholesterol 1mg
Sodium 145mg
Carbohydrate 8g
   Dietary fiber 0g
   Sugars 1g
Protein 1g

CHEDDAR-RYE BREADSTICKS

Fresh from the oven, these breadsticks are nothing to shake a stick at. Get the kids involved by having them shape the breadsticks into letters or numbers.

Makes: 12 breadsticks

Serving size: 1 breadstick

Preparation time: 2½ hours

Cooking time: 15 to 20 minutes

Ingredients

1 packet of dry yeast (¼ oz.)

1 cup warm water

1 tablespoon molasses or honey

½ teaspoon salt

1 cup rye flour

¾ cup grated reduced-fat cheddar cheese

1½ cups all-purpose flour

Cooking spray

For the glaze:

1 large egg, beaten

1 teaspoon water

2 tablespoons sesame seeds

1 In a medium-size mixing bowl, sprinkle the yeast over ¼ cup of the warm water. Stir and set aside for about 5 minutes until the yeast begins to froth. Add the remaining water, molasses or honey, salt, rye flour, and cheese, mixing well after each addition. Stir in half the all-purpose flour and as much more as needed to form a stiff dough.

2 Turn the dough out onto a lightly floured surface. Use the remaining flour, as necessary, to prevent sticking, and knead the dough until it's elastic and smooth, 5 to 10 minutes. Place in a large bowl coated with cooking spray, cover with a clean dishtowel, and set to rise in a warm place for about 1 hour until doubled in size.

3 Punch down the dough with your fist and turn out onto a lightly floured board. Divide the dough into 12 pieces and roll into 6-inch-long breadsticks. Place on a baking sheet coated with cooking spray, cover with a clean dishtowel, and set to rise in a warm place for 30 minutes.

4 Preheat the oven to 425°. In a small bowl, whisk together the egg and water and then use a pastry brush to lightly coat each breadstick. Sprinkle with the sesame seeds and bake 15 to 20 minutes until the sticks are browned and crisp. Serve immediately or transfer to a rack to cool.

NUTRITION
PER SERVING

Calories 119
Calories from fat 20
Total fat 2g
    Saturated fat 1g
Cholesterol 5mg
Sodium 158mg
Carbohydrate 20g
    Dietary fiber 2g
    Sugars 1g
Protein 5g

Sunny Days:
Picnics and Parties

SUNNY DAYS

Life's a party, and the earlier your child can feel a part of its celebrations in spite of diabetes, the better. No child should be denied the joy that comes with backyard barbecues, birthday celebrations, and kid-friendly holidays such as Halloween and Easter. In fact, when we tested the recipes on our panel of children, these recipes were the biggest hits.

This chapter is designed as three recipe menus, enabling you and your child to put together a great meal for a number of occasions. And each menu has a sweet treat, including chocolate and caramel, as a fine finish to the meal.

Best of all, these recipes really can be enjoyed at any time of the year, as they are completely diabetes-friendly. So whether the occasion is ghosts and goblins served up with Witches' Stew or a rousing chorus sung around the birthday cake, your child will certainly feel part of the gang at any party.

PICNICS AND PARTIES TABLE OF CONTENTS

WITCHES' STEW

Serves: 8

Serving size: ¾ cup

Preparation time: 15 minutes

Cooking time: 50 minutes

Ingredients

2 teaspoons olive oil

1 small onion, peeled and finely chopped

2 garlic cloves, peeled and minced

1 large carrot, peeled and diced

1 pound lean ground turkey

1 can (28 oz.) whole tomatoes, roughly chopped, with juices

1 can (14 oz.) reduced-fat, reduced-sodium chicken broth

2 tablespoons tomato paste

½ teaspoon dried oregano

½ teaspoon dried basil

¼ teaspoon dried thyme

Dash of Tabasco sauce

Salt and pepper to taste

½ cup shredded reduced-fat cheddar cheese

If you need a hot meal after trick-or-treating, here's a boiling cauldron of hearty tomato stew, spicy enough to warm even a witch on a cold night.

1 Heat the oil in a Dutch oven or large, heavy pot over medium heat. Add the onion, garlic, and carrot and cook about 8 minutes, stirring occasionally, until softened. Add the ground turkey and continue to cook, breaking up any lumps, until the meat is lightly browned, 5 to 8 minutes more.

2 Add the remaining ingredients except the cheese, stir well to combine, and bring to a boil. Reduce the heat to low and simmer about 30 minutes, stirring occasionally, until well thickened.

3 To serve, spoon into individual bowls and top with the cheese.

NUTRITION
PER SERVING

Calories 155
Calories from fat 69
Total fat 7g
    Saturated fat 2g
Cholesterol 55mg
Sodium 294mg
Carbohydrate 8g
    Dietary fiber 2g
    Sugars 5g
Protein 13g

MONSTER CARAMEL-APPLE TREATS

Serves: 8

Serving size: 1 cup

Preparation time: 10 minutes

Ingredients

2 red apples, cored and diced

2 green apples, cored and diced

2 teaspoons lemon juice

1 quart low-fat, low-sugar vanilla
frozen yogurt

½ cup sugar-free caramel
ice-cream topping

Even a ghost or a goblin is less scary when there's ice cream around. Enjoy this traditional treat served in a dessert dish.

1 In a medium-size mixing bowl combine the apples and toss with the lemon juice. Divide the mixture among eight dessert dishes. Top with a scoop of frozen yogurt and drizzle with the caramel topping. Serve immediately.

NUTRITION PER SERVING

Calories 185	Sodium 132mg
Calories from fat 41	Carbohydrate 36g
Total fat 5g	Dietary fiber 2g
Saturated fat 3g	Sugars 13g
Cholesterol 20mg	Protein 4g

Awesome Tip

Have a talk with your child about making food choices at someone else's home. Kids need to feel confident about handling the choices presented to them. Have a talk with the parents hosting the event to make sure there will be something your child can eat.

DEVILISH EGGLETS

Serves: 12

Serving size: 2 egg halves

Preparation time: 10 minutes

Cooking time: 25 minutes

Ingredients

1 dozen large eggs

½ cup reduced-fat mayonnaise

2 teaspoons dried oregano

¼ teaspoon garlic powder

4 tablespoons reduced-sodium ketchup

Chopped parsley for garnish

NUTRITION PER SERVING

Calories 97	Sodium 158mg
Calories from fat 57	Carbohydrate 3g
Total fat 6g	Dietary fiber 0
Saturated fat 2g	Sugars 2g
Cholesterol 212mg	Protein 6g

Ketchup and oregano not only add flavor, they bring a different look to this traditional dish.

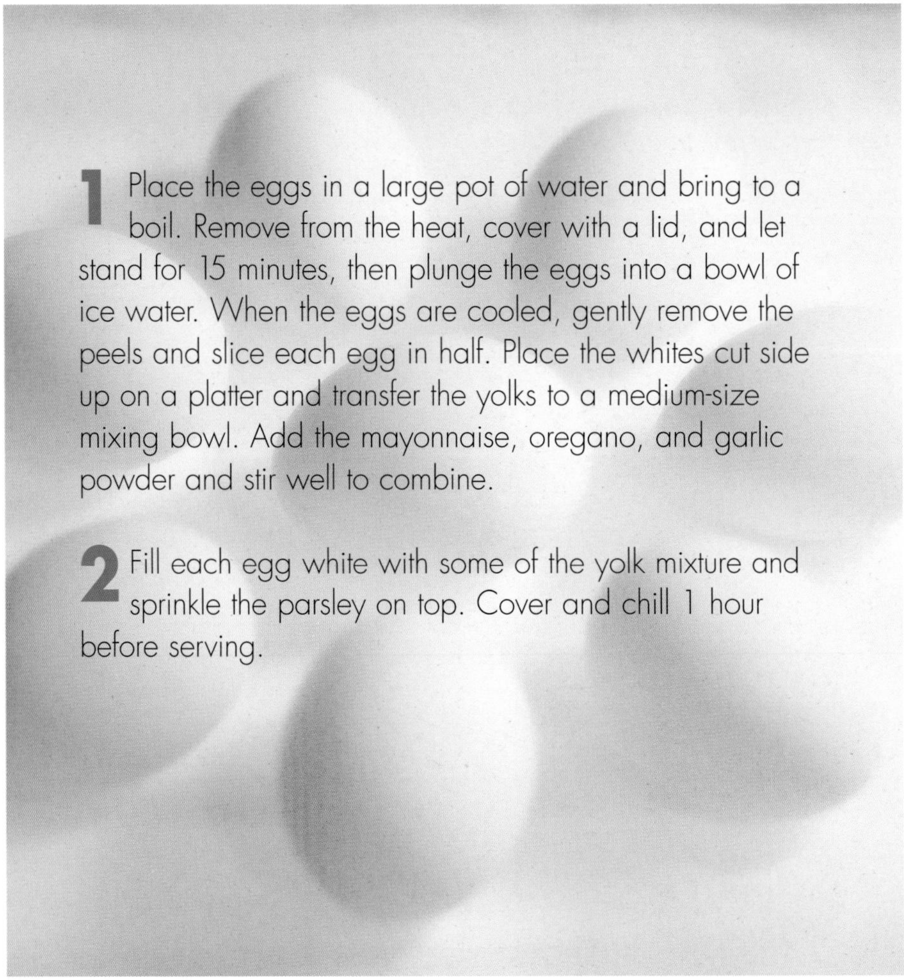

1 Place the eggs in a large pot of water and bring to a boil. Remove from the heat, cover with a lid, and let stand for 15 minutes, then plunge the eggs into a bowl of ice water. When the eggs are cooled, gently remove the peels and slice each egg in half. Place the whites cut side up on a platter and transfer the yolks to a medium-size mixing bowl. Add the mayonnaise, oregano, and garlic powder and stir well to combine.

2 Fill each egg white with some of the yolk mixture and sprinkle the parsley on top. Cover and chill 1 hour before serving.

SURPRISE-INSIDE JUICY TURKEY BURGERS

Serves: 8

Serving size: 1 burger (4 oz.)

Preparation time: 12 minutes

Cooking time: 10 to 12 minutes

Ingredients

½ pound ground turkey breast

½ pound lean ground beef

1 teaspoon garlic powder

½ teaspoon onion powder

Salt and pepper to taste

4 cubes (1 oz. each) reduced-fat cheddar cheese

4 small whole-wheat buns, split

4 tomato slices (optional)

4 lettuce leaves (optional)

NUTRITION PER SERVING

Calories 407	Sodium 589
Calories from fat 154	Carbohydrate 25g
Total fat 17g	Dietary fiber 4g
Saturated fat 8g	Sugars 5g
Cholesterol 116mg	Protein 38g

Warm melted cheese inside these burgers makes for a really cool treat. Add your favorite condiment to personalize yours.

1 Preheat an oven broiler or outdoor grill to medium-high.

2 In a medium-size mixing bowl, combine the turkey, beef, garlic powder, onion powder, salt, and pepper and mix well. Divide into eight patties, place the cheese cube on four of them, and top with the remaining patties, pressing down to securely enclose the cheese.

3 Broil or grill the burgers about 6 minutes per side until well browned and cooked through.

4 Serve on the buns with the tomato and lettuce, if desired, and condiments of choice.

SEESAW APPLE COLESLAW

Serves: 6

Serving size: ¾ cup

Preparation time: 15 minutes

Ingredients

2 cups finely shredded green cabbage

1 cup finely shredded red cabbage

1 large carrot, peeled and grated

1 Granny Smith apple, diced

¼ cup raisins

For the dressing:

½ cup reduced-fat mayonnaise

1 tablespoon apple cider vinegar

2 teaspoons honey

Dash ground cinnamon

Salt and pepper to taste

All coleslaw is not created equal. Raisins and an apple add just the right amount of sweetness to this version of your backyard-barbecue favorite.

1 In a large mixing bowl, combine the cabbages, carrots, apple, and raisins.

2 In a small mixing bowl, whisk together the dressing ingredients. Add to the cabbage mixture and toss well. Chill 1 hour before serving.

NUTRITION PER SERVING

Calories 98	Cholesterol 0
Calories from fat 28	Sodium 258mg
Total fat 3g	Carbohydrate 18g
Saturated fat 1g	Dietary fiber 2g
	Sugars 13g
	Protein 1g

ALL-AMERICAN ICE-CREAM FLOATS

Who can resist an ice-cream float? And who can resist raspberries? Keep this mixture on hand for a quick dessert anytime.

Serves: 4

Serving size: 1cup

Preparation time: 8 minutes

Ingredients

1 cup fresh or frozen raspberries

1½ teaspoons sugar

2 cups light vanilla ice cream

3 cups club soda

NUTRITION PER SERVING

Calories 123	Sodium 100mg
Calories from fat 45	Carbohydrate 19g
Total fat 5g	Dietary fiber 1
Saturated fat 2.5g	Sugars 7g
Cholesterol 18mg	Protein 3g

1 Press the raspberries through a sieve over a small bowl and discard the seeds. Combine the raspberry pulp and sugar and stir well.

2 Divide the raspberry mixture evenly among 4 tall glasses or parfait glasses.

3 Spoon ¼ cup of ice cream into each glass. Stir in 2 tablespoons of club soda, and top with the remaining ice cream. Pour the rest of the club soda over and serve immediately.

CHICKEN CAESAR SALAD BOATS

Sail away with this salad in a sandwich. It makes a yummy and quick lunch even without the bun.

Serves: 4

Serving size: 1 sandwich

Preparation time: 5 minutes

Ingredients

4 whole-wheat buns

2 cups cooked chicken strips, such as Perdue's Shortcuts

½ cup reduced-fat Caesar salad dressing

2 tablespoons grated Parmesan cheese

1 cup shredded romaine lettuce

½ cup fat-free croutons, slightly crushed

1 Cut the buns in half. Scoop out the bread from the center of the bottom half, reserving for another use, if desired.

2 In a medium-size mixing bowl, combine the chicken, dressing, and cheese, and toss well to coat.

3 Divide the lettuce among the bottom halves of the buns. Top with the chicken salad and then the croutons. Top with remaining bun halves and serve immediately.

NUTRITION PER SERVING

Calories 303	Sodium 607mg
Calories from fat 54	Carbohydrate 31g
Total fat 6g	Dietary fiber 4g
Saturated fat 1g	Sugars 9g
Cholesterol 64mg	Protein 26g

CRINKLY VEGETABLES WITH
CREAMY MUSTARD-PARMESAN DIP

The cheese in this dip really adds to the zip of the mustard. Go crazy with any veggies you want and display them on a fun platter. Instant party!

Serves: 6

Serving size: 2 tablespoons

Preparation time: 11 minutes

Ingredients

2 medium-size carrots, peeled and sliced with a crinkle cutter

1 small zucchini, trimmed and sliced with a crinkle cutter

1 small yellow squash, trimmed and sliced with a crinkle cutter

½ medium-size cucumber, peeled and sliced with a crinkle cutter

For the dip:

½ cup low-fat mayonnaise

¼ cup grated Parmesan cheese

2 tablespoons Dijon mustard

1 teaspoon onion powder

1 teaspoon garlic powder

1 Arrange the cut vegetables in rows on a platter.

2 In a small bowl, stir together all the ingredients for the dip.

3 Serve the dip with the vegetables.

NUTRITION
PER SERVING

Calories 90
Calories from fat 47
Total fat 5g
    Saturated fat 2g
Cholesterol 6mg
Sodium 421mg
Carbohydrate 8g
    Dietary fiber 1.5g
    Sugars 4g
Protein 4g

IN-THE-GOOD-OLD-SUMMERTIME FRUIT SALAD

Crunchy vanilla wafers turn this regular salad into an extraordinary treat.
Keep the cookies separate until you're ready to serve.

Serves: 4

Serving size: ½ cup

Preparation time: 15 minutes

1 In a medium-size mixing bowl, gently combine all the fruits and keep refrigerated.

2 To serve, dish out the fruit and top with the crushed cookies.

Ingredients

½ cup fresh blueberries

½ cup sliced strawberries

½ cup diced fresh peaches

½ cup diced nectarines

½ cup crushed sugar-free vanilla wafer cookies (about 8)

NUTRITION PER SERVING

Calories 80	Sodium 19mg
Calories from fat 26	Carbohydrate 14g
Total fat 3g	Dietary fiber 3g
Saturated fat .5g	Sugars 8g
Cholesterol 0	Protein 1g

BIGFOOT SUBMARINE SANDWICH

This turkey sub is big enough to feed any hungry crew and super delicious, to boot.

Serves: 10

Serving size: 1 sandwich slice

Preparation time: 25 minutes

Ingredients

1 loaf French bread (16 oz.), split lengthwise

⅔ cup fat-free ranch-style dressing

2 cups shredded romaine lettuce

2 medium-size carrots, peeled and shredded

3 medium-size tomatoes, thinly sliced

1½ pounds low-salt roast turkey breast, thinly sliced

1 Spread one side of the bread with the ranch-style dressing.

2 Layer the lettuce, carrots, tomatoes, and turkey over the dressing. Top with the remaining bread.

3 Place ten frilled toothpicks at intervals and slice between them. Arrange the slices on a large platter and serve immediately or cover with plastic wrap and refrigerate up to 3 hours.

NUTRITION PER SERVING

Calories 217	Sodium 575mg
Calories from fat 28	Carbohydrate 32g
Total fat 3g	Dietary fiber 2g
Saturated fat 1g	Sugars 5
Cholesterol 26mg	Protein 16g

OH, SO STRAWBERRY CHOCOLATE ICE-CREAM CAKE

Chocolate-dipped strawberries are wonderful on their own, but they can't compare to this ice-cream cake. And if it isn't decadent enough, just drizzle some syrup on top!

Serves: 10

Serving size: 1 slice (1-inch)

Preparation time: 30 minutes
Freeze for 12 hours

Cooking time: 25 minutes

Ingredients

Cooking spray

1 box (20 oz.) low-fat brownie mix

1 quart reduced-fat, sugar-free vanilla ice cream or frozen yogurt, softened

2 cups chopped fresh strawberries

½ cup sugar-free, fat-free chocolate or butterscotch syrup

1 Preheat the oven to 350°. Coat two 8-inch round cake pans with cooking spray and dust lightly with flour.

2 Prepare the brownie mix according to the package directions, dividing the batter between the two pans. Bake about 25 minutes until set.

3 Cool the brownie cakes in the pan for 10 to 15 minutes, then invert onto racks to cool completely.

4 Line one of the cleaned cake pans with foil, overlapping the sides, and place one cake in the bottom. Spread the ice cream evenly over the cake and top with the strawberries. Place the other cake on top of the berries and ice cream and press firmly. Fold over the foil to cover and freeze overnight.

5 Just before serving, unfold the top foil and use it to lift up the cake, transferring it to a platter. Use a serrated knife to cut the cake into 10 slices and serve each portion with a drizzle of syrup on top.

NUTRITION PER SERVING	
Calories 345	Sodium 389mg
Calories from fat 41	Carbohydrate 35g
Total fat 5g	Dietary fiber 2g
Saturated fat 2g	Sugars 17g
Cholesterol 14mg	Protein 5g

Awesome Tip: It's all about balance, not deprivation. Teach your child that a small piece of cake is permissible but it means that the rest of that day's food will have to be balanced. Work with a registered dietitian who understands how to keep a food program flexible.

PEANUT-BUTTER-AND-APPLE CELERY BOATS

Serves: 10

Serving size: 2 celery boats

Preparation time: 10 minutes

Ingredients

⅔ cup reduced-fat peanut butter

1 red delicious apple, peeled, cored, and grated

½ teaspoon cinnamon

10 medium to large celery stalks, trimmed and peeled

NUTRITION PER SERVING

Calories 125	Sodium 114
Calories from fat 58	Carbohydrate 11g
Total fat 6g	Dietary fiber 3g
Saturated fat 1g	Sugars 3g
Cholesterol 0	Protein 5g

We've all tried peanut butter and celery, but grated apple is the secret ingredient that really adds a zip to this classic treat.

1 In a small mixing bowl, combine the peanut butter, grated apple, and cinnamon.

2 Cut each celery stalk crosswise into two pieces and stuff each piece with some of the peanut-butter mixture.
Serve immediately or cover and refrigerate up to 4 hours.

Awesome Tip: Stuffed veggies for a snack are downright fun! Kids will love the stuffing process, and they get the bonus of good nutrition. Use any of the dips in this chapter as a stuffing. Here are some examples:

• **Cherry Tomato Cups:** Remove the stems and cut a thin slice from the tops. Carefully scoop out the seeds and flesh, leaving the outside intact. Lightly salt the insides of the tomatoes to draw out excess moisture. Invert on a rack to drain for 10 minutes before stuffing.

VALENTINE'S DAY MUFFIN PIZZAS

Kids can assemble their own versions of this pizza. Serve it with a variety of cheeses cut into heart shapes along with other toppings such as mushrooms.

Serves: 2

Serving size: 1 muffin

Preparation time: 5 minutes

Cooking time: 6 to 8 minutes

Ingredients

2 whole-grain English muffins, split

½ cup marinara sauce

1 sliced reduced-sodium pepperoni (4 oz.)

4 slices (1 oz. each) reduced-fat cheese

1 Preheat the oven to 400°.

2 Spread each muffin half with the sauce and top with pepperoni. Using a 2½-inch-wide heart-shaped cookie cutter, make a cheese heart for each pizza and place it on top of the pepperoni.

3 Transfer the muffin pizzas to a baking sheet and bake 6 to 8 minutes until the cheese melts and the muffin is crisp. Serve immediately.

NUTRITION PER SERVING

Calories 214	Sodium 590mg
Calories from fat 54	Carbohydrate 19g
Total fat 6g	Dietary fiber 3g
Saturated fat 2g	Sugars 3g
Cholesterol 40mg	Protein 21g

• **Cucumber Cups:** Using a fork, score the skin of a cucumber lengthwise. Cut crosswise into ¾-inch slices. Using a melon-baller or teaspoon, scoop out the flesh from each slice, leaving a ¼-inch shell. Lightly salt the cups and invert them on a rack to drain for 10 minutes before stuffing.

• **Snow Pea Purses:** Blanch snow peas in boiling water for 30 seconds. Plunge into cold water and drain. Carefully slit open the curved side of each pod and stuff.

SWEETHEART STRAWBERRY FIZZ

This drink is the perfect kids' "mocktail" for any occasion. Ginger ale adds the right amount of sweet-and-bubbly.

Serves: 4

Serving size: ½ cup

Preparation time: 8 minutes

Ingredients

- 1 cup no-sugar-added frozen strawberries, slightly thawed

- 1 kiwi fruit, peeled and cut into chunks

- 1 cup diet ginger ale

1 Purée the strawberries and kiwi fruit in a blender, using a bit of the ginger ale, if necessary, to blend. Pour into 4 glasses and fill with the remaining ginger ale.

NUTRITION PER SERVING

Calories 25	Carbohydrate 6g
Total fat 0	Dietary fiber 1g
Cholesterol 0	Sugars 3g
Sodium 16mg	Protein 0

DE-LIGHTFUL, DE-LOVELY RASPBERRY BROWNIES

Chocolate and jam make this a sweet treat that you can whip up as a quick dessert for any occasion. Try your own version with different sugar-free jams and jellies.

Makes: 24 brownie hearts

Serving size: 1 heart

Preparation time: 15 minutes

Cooking time: 30 minutes

Ingredients

Cooking spray

1 box (20 oz.) low-fat brownie mix

½ cup sugar-free raspberry jam

Confectioners' sugar for dusting

1 Preheat the oven to 350°. Coat one square 8 x 8-inch baking pan with cooking spray. Dust lightly with flour.

2 Prepare the brownie mix according to package directions. Pour half the batter in the pan, swirl in the raspberry jam, and cover with the remaining batter. Bake according to package directions.

3 Transfer the pan to a wire rack and allow to cool completely. Using 2 spatulas, remove the brownie from the pan in one piece and place on a cutting board. Use a small 1-inch-wide heart-shaped cookie cutter to make 24 brownies. Transfer to a serving platter and sprinkle with the confectioners' sugar.

NUTRITION
PER SERVING

Calories 103
Calories from fat 3
Total fat .5g
    Saturated fat 0
Cholesterol 0
Sodium 129mg
Carbohydrate 24g
    Dietary fiber 0
    Sugars 17g
Protein 1g

EASTER-BUNNY FRITTATA WITH CHEESE

Even if your kids don't find all the Easter eggs, they won't want to miss this savory breakfast. Garlic, onion, and cheese add so much flavor to this egg dish – everyone will want seconds!

Serves: 6

Serving size: ⅙ of frittata

Preparation time: 16 minutes

Cooking time: 18 to 20 minutes

Ingredients

- 2 teaspoons olive oil
- 1 garlic clove, peeled and minced
- 1 small onion, peeled and finely chopped
- 1 cup small broccoli florets
- 2 large eggs
- 4 large egg whites
- ¼ cup grated Parmesan cheese
- ½ cup shredded reduced-fat cheddar cheese
- 1 tablespoon all-purpose flour
- ½ teaspoon dried basil
- Salt and pepper to taste

1 In a large broiler-proof skillet, heat 1 teaspoon of the oil over medium-high heat. Add the garlic, onion, and broccoli and cook about 3 minutes, stirring often, until somewhat softened. Using a slotted spoon, remove the vegetables from the skillet and set aside.

2 In a large mixing bowl, whisk together the eggs, egg whites, Parmesan and cheddar cheeses, flour, basil, salt, and pepper until well combined. Fold in the onions, garlic, and broccoli.

3 Heat the remaining oil in the skillet over medium heat. Pour in the egg mixture and cook without stirring for 10 minutes until it's set around the edges. Preheat the broiler.

4 Broil the frittata in the skillet about 6 inches from the heat source until the top and center of the frittata are set, 1 to 2 minutes. Carefully remove the skillet with oven gloves and cut into 6 equal portions. Serve immediately.

NUTRITION
PER SERVING

Calories 105
Calories from fat 50
Total fat 6g
 Saturated fat 3g
Cholesterol 74mg
Sodium 210mg
Carbohydrate 4g
 Dietary fiber 1g
 Sugars 1g
Protein 8g

BUNNY SALAD

Any bunny would be proud of this salad. It's a sweet yet healthful side dish that combines carrots and apples with just the right amount of raisins and cinnamon.

Serves: 6

Serving size: ¾ cup

Preparation time: 45 minutes

Ingredients

4 large carrots, peeled and shredded

1 small apple, cored and diced

½ cup raisins

For the dressing:

½ cup low-fat mayonnaise

2 teaspoons lemon juice

½ teaspoon cinnamon

Salt and pepper to taste

1 In a medium-size mixing bowl, combine the carrots, apples, and raisin. In a small mixing bowl, whisk together the dressing ingredients and add to the salad, stirring well to coat. Cover and refrigerate for 30 minutes before serving.

NUTRITION PER SERVING

Calories 103	Sodium 232mg
Calories from fat 26	Carbohydrate 21g
Total fat 3g	Dietary fiber 3g
Saturated fat 1g	Sugars 13g
Cholesterol 0	Protein 1g

EGGS-OF-A-DIFFERENT-COLOR DESSERT TREATS

Makes: 28 treats

Serving size: 2

Preparation time: 20 minutes

Cooking time: 3 hours

Ingredients

Cooking spray

6 large egg whites, at room temperature

¼ teaspoon salt

¼ teaspoon cream of tartar

½ cup Splenda for baking

½ teaspoon vanilla extract

Assorted food colorings

Eggs are among the most versatile foods, and here they are the basis of a delicious meringue dessert that tastes like cotton candy in a cookie.

1 Preheat the oven to 200°. Coat a large baking sheet with cooking spray.

2 In a large mixing bowl, using an electric mixer set on high speed, beat the egg whites with the salt and cream of tartar until soft peaks form. Continue beating on high while gradually adding the Splenda, 2 tablespoons at a time. Add the vanilla and beat until stiff, glossy peaks have formed.

3 Divide the beaten eggs whites into 3 or 4 small mixing bowls and color each batch with a drop or two of food coloring, stirring well to combine.

4 Mound the mixture on the baking sheet, forming oval egg shapes. Bake about 3 hours until the outsides of the meringues are crisp. Remove from the oven and cool completely on the baking sheet. To store, wrap the meringues loosely in waxed paper in a covered container. Keep at room temperature.

NUTRITION PER SERVING	
Calories 12	Carbohydrate 1g
Total fat 0	Dietary fiber 0
Cholesterol 0	Sugars 0
Sodium 66mg	Protein 2g

Resources

The following works were consulted in the writing and preparation of this book.

Betty Page Brackenridge, M.S., R.D., C.D.E. and Richard Rubin, Ph.D., C.D.E., *Sweet Kids: How to Balance Diabetes Control and Good Nutrition with Family Peace*, American Diabetes Association, 2002

Better Homes and Gardens and Jan Miller, editors, *Kid Favorites Made Healthy*, Meredith Books, 2003

Linda M Siminerio, R.N., Ph.D., C.D.E. and Jean Betschart, M.N., M.S.N., C.P.N.P., C.D.E., *Guide to Raising a Child with Diabetes*, American Diabetes Association, 2000

Robyn Webb, editor, *Eat to Beat Diabetes*, Reader's Digest Books, 2003

Tim Wysocki, Ph.D., *The Ten Keys to Helping Your Child Grow Up with Diabetes*, American Diabetes Association, 2004

Index

Other books from Cleveland Clinic Press

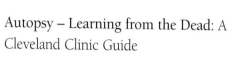

Age Well! A Cleveland Clinic Guide

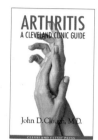

Arthritis: A Cleveland Clinic Guide

Autopsy – Learning from the Dead: A Cleveland Clinic Guide

Battling the Beast Within: Success in Living with Adversity (about multiple sclerosis)

Breastless in the City: A Young Woman's Story of Love, Loss, and Breast Cancer

Forever Home (a chapter book about homelessness and loss for young readers)

Getting a Good Night's Sleep: A Cleveland Clinic Guide

The Granny-Nanny: A Guide for Parents and Grandparents Who Share Child Care

Heart Attack: A Cleveland Clinic Guide

Heroes with a Thousand Faces: True Stories of People with Facial Deformities and their Quest for Acceptance